IRON TOOTHPICK

A Thru-Hiker Reveals Life, Legends and Oddities along the Appalachian Trail

IRON TOOTHPICK

A Thru-Hiker Reveals Life, Legends and Oddities along the Appalachian Trail

Andy Harrah

Rainmaker Publishing LLC
Oakton, Virginia, USA

ISBN: 0-9765498-3-2
LCCN: 2006921039

⊗ Printed on Acid-Free Paper
Printing: Automated Graphic Systems — White Plains, Maryland
Book Design: Dianne Harrah, Wolf Run Studio — Clifton, Virginia

Rainmaker Publishing LLC
Oakton, Virginia
info@rainmakerpublishing.com
www.rainmakerpublishing.com

Acknowledgements

When I started my hike, the Appalachian Trail was simply a very long trail. Now, I know the trail to be a large community of kind and generous people, set in a lush green wilderness. I'd like to thank all of those in the Appalachian Trail community who selflessly offer their time and energy to host a new wave of adventurers every year. The trail is a very special place, and it is because of you.

Pete and Michaela, thank you for your tireless logistical support. Knowing that I could have anything I wished mailed to me with just a phone call, gave me enormous flexibility. Thank you for your patience, your time, and all of the homemade cookies. If my hike was nothing else, I'm happy that it served as an ice breaker to what has become a cherished friendship.

Mom and Dad, thank you for your love, and support and for raising me to become an independent, confident and happy adult.

Hoser, Wild Flamingo, Mr. Ed and Tang, I had a great summer hanging out with you. Thank you all for the good conversations, good laughs, and good times. I hope you enjoy the book.

Iron Toothpick

Note to Readers

The events depicted and views expressed in this book solely reflect the perspective and opinions of the author and do not necessarily represent the opinions of the publisher. With respect to private individuals named in the book (as contrasted to those associated with a commercial business or establishment that solicits a fee or donation in exchange for services) every attempt was made to obtain permission to name these individuals. In the event such permission was not obtained, names have been changed to protect their privacy.

Table of Contents

The End Is Near

THE END IS NEAR

Tomorrow is my last day on the Appalachian Trail (AT). Five months of hiking have brought me to the base of Katahdin Mountain in Maine. As I go to sleep tonight, only 6 of the 2,172 miles of trail remain before me.

My goal in April was clear; to hike the AT from end to end in one season. Time has flown by and I feel as if I was in Georgia only a short time ago. At the same time, I cannot see how I can have so many memories from less than half a year. Somewhere, between Georgia and Maine, hiking the AT became much more about the journey than the destination.

People stand out the most. There is Windtalker, who was the first thru-hiker I got to know. Hoser, Mr. Ed and Wild Flamingo, who I hiked several hundred miles with and was happy to bring to my home for a few days in June. The family in New York who invited a bunch of smelly hiking strangers to their lake home for a Fourth of July cookout that I will never forget; and Jump'n and Tang, whom I've hiked all of Maine with and are here camping with me tonight.

Be Careful What You Read

MY INTEREST IN HIKING the AT started innocently enough. I was killing time in a bookstore, browsing my usual sports and outdoor sections, when I came across a book called *Long Distance Hiking: Lessons from the Appalachian Trail* by Roland Mueser. Being a fan of adventure, I started thumbing through it. The book was a bit dated since Mueser hiked the AT more than ten years earlier, but it included a good mix of facts and statistics on the AT which appealed to my analytical side. There were details about all aspects of long distance hiking, including what type of gear to use like stoves, tents and hiking boots as well as strategies for re-supplying along the trail. Standing there between "Eastern Philosophy" and "Self Help," I read a quarter of it.

I grew up and still live in Northern Virginia. I knew a little about the AT since it passes within 40 miles of my home, but probably not more than most people who live in the area. I knew that the trail was about 2,000 miles, it stretched from Georgia to Maine and every year some people took many months to hike it in its entirety. These are just facts I knew, but I never heard the AT calling to me personally.

I'm a runner and a triathlete, but I was never really much of a backpacker or camper. I went on the occasional camping trip as a Boy Scout, and although I like the outdoors, my memories of backpacking were of blistered feet and aching shoulders. While reading Mueser's book, I thought about the physical pain long-distance hikers must endure after weeks and months on the AT. The discomfort I considered unbearable after just a few days, must be what these people live with for months.

I purchased the book, and over the next few months I referred to it as questions about the AT popped into my head. For some reason, I became more and more curious about the logistics of making such an epic hike. Some of the first questions I had were: What kind of food do people bring? How much gear do they carry? How long does the entire hike take? What is the best type of tent to bring? Can you bring a stove? While searching for answers to my questions in Mueser's book, I made discoveries that surprised me.

I learned that there is a large community of hikers on the trail every summer and that many hikers only spend a handful of nights camping alone. I also learned that some hikers spend many nights in hotels, re-supply points occur frequently and at least a few hikers only carry a daypack instead of a full-sized backpack. The thing that appealed to me most was that a couple of hikers surveyed in the book hiked in running shoes. Hiking in running shoes and carrying only a daypack made hiking the trail seem feasible, although it was just a thought exercise for me at the time.

Slowly, the information I learned fed daydreams about what a typical day would be like for me if I hiked the trail. I thought about how many hours I would hike a day, if I would hike alone or with other people I met along the way and where I would sleep. I envisioned a very simple daily routine of waking up, packing my gear and hiking all day with a few meals along the way. The idea of such a simple existence began to grow on me. Hiking the trail seemed like it might be a socially acceptable way to just be.

After a few months, I seriously began to consider hiking the trail myself. I mulled these thoughts around for a few days before sharing my idea with anyone. Finally, one morning during a routine eight-mile run with my friend Tracey, I mentioned my idea of hiking the AT. By telling Tracey, I was actually taking a survey and her response could have killed my idea and deprived me of one of the best experiences of my life. Lucky for me, Tracey thought that hiking the AT was a good idea.

Next, I told my girlfriend at the time about the idea. She didn't know anything about the AT, so I filled her in with what I had learned. She asked all the normal questions: How long is it? Do you hike the entire way without stopping? How long will it take? Are you crazy?

My girlfriend thought that hiking the AT was a bit ridiculous and couldn't believe anyone actually did it. But, being supportive, she started to learn about it and soon became an expert of sorts despite the fact that she thought the idea was silly. Little by little though, she found out that hiking the AT was quite popular and that not only had many people heard of it, but for a few it was their dream to hike the entire length. Gradually, in her eyes, hiking the AT became cool.

Next, I floated the idea at work. I had worked as a software engineer for 12 years and had never taken an extended leave of absence. Knowing that taking multiple consecutive months off was a pretty big deal, I asked for time off 18 months in advance. The people at work shared my girlfriend's initial skepticism. Assuming, however, that my interest in hiking the AT was just a phase I would get over before my actual departure date arrived, they gave me the "okay" to take the time off. Things were falling into place.

Prepare, Prepare, Prepare

I DID A LOT OF RESEARCH to prepare for my hike on the AT. There is no shortage of information on the Internet about the trail from hiking clubs, conservation organizations and journals from people who have hiked the trail themselves.

The Appalachian Trail Conservancy (ATC) in Harpers Ferry, West Virginia, is a private, 80-year-old organization made up of volunteers who are dedicated to the conservation of the AT. The organization coordinates the trail's management and protection and works with numerous groups, including the National Park Service's Appalachian Trail Park Office, to protect the trail so that people can enjoy it for years to come. In addition to the ATC, there are 30 clubs that volunteer to maintain the footpath.

In 1948, Earl Shaffer became the first person to hike the entire length of the AT. Only a few people each year over the next 20 years followed in his footsteps. By 1970, only 70 people had completed what is known as a "thru-hike" of the AT, by hiking the trail from end to end. In contrast, today over 400 hikers complete a thru-hike every year.

Emma Gatewood, who was a grandmother of 23 and also known on the trail as "Grandma Gatewood," thru-hiked the trail in the 1950s. What set Emma apart from other early hikers was the approach she took to her gear. Emma was the first "ultralight" hiker. She hiked in tennis shoes, used a shower curtain as a rain tarp and her rain cape doubled as her ground cloth. Her ultralight approach didn't become popular until more than 40 years later when people started replacing traditional heavy hiking gear with lightweight equipment and clothing.

I soon learned through my research that what was revolutionary in Mueser's book, is now commonplace. Nearly everyone hikes the AT in running shoes and carries less than 40 pounds in their pack. There are also a lot of lightweight gear options to choose from for almost every piece of equipment you need.

I spent hours looking at hiking and camping gear and decided that I would sleep in a lightweight hammock, wear trail running shoes and carry everything in what essentially amounted to a duffel bag with shoulder straps. I was determined to hike with as little weight as possible, and even chose my watch based on weight. The only thing I had trouble finding was a camping stove that was light enough to meet my newly forming "thru-hiker" standards, so I decided to make my own stove out of a single cat food can. This took more than a little trial and error, but it was worth the trouble and weight reduction. I chose a single titanium pot to accompany it and used my titanium tent stakes to perform double duty as a pot stand. With a little innovation, I ended up with a very lightweight "kitchen" that served me well during my hike.

While researching equipment that past thru-hikers used on the trail, I discovered PocketMail®. PocketMail, as it sounds, is a small device that would enable me to send and receive email from any telephone, including payphones. I could write my trail journal on it as I hiked, then send the journal entries and email to friends and family back home. I could also receive email this way. I was sold on the idea, and purchased the PocketMail device.

There are two obvious ways to thru-hike the AT, northbound and southbound. There are also a few people who begin in Georgia, hike a portion of the trail going northbound, then take a bus to the northern terminus of the trail in Maine, and hike south to where they left the trail. I decided to join the majority of thru-hikers and start in Georgia and hike northbound to Maine. This would allow me to begin my hike early in the spring and complete it in early fall, before the weather turned cold in Maine.

The volunteer clubs that maintain the trail also maintain camping shelters for hikers. Most of the shelters are very basic and consist of a rectangular floor, a back wall, two side walls and a roof that is pitched toward the back of the shelter. The fronts of the shelters are completely open and most are located near a water source and have a privy. In most places, shelters are located 8 to 12 miles apart.

Everything I read indicated that the shelters in Georgia would be crowded since so many people begin their thru-hikes in the spring like I had planned. Space in shelters sounded like it was claimed on a first-come, first-served basis.

Most shelters have a register; which is really just a spiral notebook. Hikers write notes in the registers when they stop for the night or for a break during the day. Some people write jokes or messages to other hikers, while others just document that they were there.

There are also hostels along the trail, most which sprung up specifically to serve thru-hikers. At a minimum, hostels provide showers and a dry place to sleep. Beyond that, the services vary, but most either have or will shuttle hikers to a laundry facility and a store to re-supply. Most hostels either charge a small fee or request a donation from their guests. The people who own the hostels along the AT are known for their generosity, and as it turned out, my experience on the trail was as much defined by the people as by the footpath itself.

In my research, I found many references to the *Appalachian Trail Data Book*, also called the *Data Book*. I found this book through the ATC and decided to order a current copy to see what everyone was talking about.

The *Data Book* is a yearly publication that is about the size of a small notepad and can easily fit into your pocket. It has 75 pages of information that seemed indispensable to a thru-hiker, including a list of camp sites, camping shelters, water sources and major features from the start of the trail at Springer Mountain in Georgia to Mount Katahdin in Maine. The book also lists the mileage between each feature as well as major road crossings. For each road crossing, the book lists the types of services that are within a reasonable distance to the trail.

Most people seemed to carry the *Data Book* on the trail with them. I scanned my first copy beginning to end, and then bought the latest version just prior to starting my hike. The book is a great resource, but lacks many helpful details. A second book, the *Appalachian Trail Thru-Hiker's Companion,* is produced by the Appalachian Trail Long Distance Hikers Association and complements the *Data Book*. The *Companion* is much larger, about 220 pages, and provides the details lacking in the *Data Book*.

An example of the difference in the two books is the type of information listed for stores near road crossings. The *Companion* lists the names, hours, phone numbers and addresses of each store as well as information on the types of stores (such as a large grocery store, or a small general store that is closed on weekends). In comparison, the *Data Book* might simply state that you can re-supply at a store located one mile from the trail. I found that the two books work together and make on-the-fly logistical planning very simple without the stress of too many surprises.

The majority of the trail sounded like it was well maintained and very well marked. The AT follows the ridge of the Appalachian Mountains and has frequent but short climbs and descents. The pictures I saw of it indicated that much of the trail was through the woods, with occasional vistas overlooking the mountains and surrounding area. It looked very inviting.

While preparing for my hike, I also learned about the trail's culture. Nearly everyone used a "trail name," which is a nickname you either give yourself or other hikers give you. Some people's names describe something about them or who they want to be when they finish the trail, while others are just fun names or names that other hikers made up. I couldn't find any information on how the tradition of trail names originated, but today it continues on its own inertia. I decided to start hiking the trail with my own name and figured that at some point I would get a new name along the way.

As my departure drew near, time seemed to stand still. I planned to start my hike on April 1, but by the beginning of March I was itching to go. I almost reconsidered my start date several times as I thought of the hundreds of hikers already out on the trail. If I got fired from my job for day-dreaming before my last day, I would have taken the next flight to Georgia.

Before I left Virginia, some friends threw a going away party for me. My obsession with carrying as little weight as possible on the trail was well known, so for a going away present, I was given a cinderblock that everyone had signed.

Amicalola Falls State Park

April Fool

THE ODDEST FEELING I had as I departed for the AT, was the realization that I was unemployed (at least for the time being). I was 33 and it was the first time since college that I did not have a job. It was an unsettling feeling, but was soon trumped by pre-trail anxiety. My absolute biggest concern was that my flight to Georgia would be delayed. This was ridiculous and I knew it. Why worry about a short delay in a trip that would take five months? I was eager to go.

As is turned out, my trip to the start of the AT couldn't have gone smoother. I flew into Atlanta on an early flight and met Tony who was waiting for me at the airport. Tony ran a shuttle service and routinely shuttled hikers from the airport to Amicalola Falls State Park, where Springer Mountain is located. I arranged a ride with Tony through email and he arrived as planned.

By noon I was in Amicalola Falls State Park on the approach to Springer Mountain. Before dropping me off, Tony told me he was available to shuttle people back to the airport from anywhere along the AT in Georgia. In a typical year, only 15 percent of the people that start hiking the AT finish, and 20 percent quit before they get out of Georgia. Tony knew the odds and offered me his business card.

I spent the first afternoon of my vacation hiking though the park to the start of the AT.

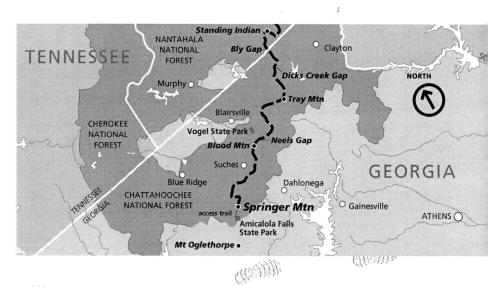

FIGHTING HIKERS TONIGHT ON SPRINGER

The hike from Amicalola Falls State Park to the top of Springer Mountain was pleasant and uneventful.

At the top of Springer Mountain I found a bunch of people getting ready to start their own hikes. One of them took the traditional photos of me with the plaque that marks the southern end of the AT.

As I got my camera out, another guy told me that after I take my pictures, he'd give me the gadget lecture. I had heard that cell phones were frowned upon on the trail, but cameras? Give me a break. This community seems like it might have more than a few rules, betraying their carefree stereotype.

The lecture turned out to be about bears, shelters, trash, etc. not gadgets. The best I can figure is that the guy's trail name is Gadget.

It was getting late, so I decided to camp near the shelter on top of the mountain. A few other people were there and more were arriving. I started setting up my hammock and a few others set up their tents nearby.

While we were setting up, Gadget walked up and told us that we were in the old tent pads, and that because of bear problems we had to camp at new pads about 200 feet away. No big deal. While we were moving our gear, Gadget continued to go on and on about why we had to move.

Finally, a guy named John said what we were all thinking, "Enough already, we're moving." John then added a few choice words. Gadget, who on the surface seemed like a calm peaceful type, snapped back at John and they both proceeded to fill the woods with yelling. Luckily, there were no chairs to throw.

The new tent sites were at the very top of the mountain and were pretty deluxe. But what seemed great at first, soon turned ugly as I learned one of the more annoying drawbacks of my hammock. It was very windy and the fly over my hammock, which gets a little loose when I get into the hammock, began flapping and kept me awake.

At midnight, I finally took the fly off. That quieted things down a bit, and I was able to fall asleep.

It was my first day on the trail, and I was witness to a screaming match that nearly turned into a fistfight. Fortunately, that event proved to be a singular one.

It turned out that a group of volunteers called Ridge Runners work each summer to help hikers enjoy the AT and to spread helpful lessons on how to preserve the nature of the trail. They are each assigned to different sections of the trail and are formally trained. They also carry radios and can call for medical assistance when necessary and deliver urgent messages to hikers at most points on the trail. If your family calls the ATC with an emergency message, a Ridge Runner will try to track you down and deliver the message. Some Ridge Runners, like Gadget, volunteer to spend a week at Springer Mountain greeting new crops of potential thru-hikers.

The next morning I formally started my hike on the AT. My goal on my first real day was to hike from Springer Mountain seven miles to the Hawk Mountain shelter. Much of the advice I heard before I left for Georgia was to start out slow on the trail to allow your feet and legs the chance to get used to hiking every day. My goal was to hike between 8 and 12 miles a day in Georgia, and then re-evaluate my mileage, depending on how my body was reacting to its new demands.

It was great to finally be on my way. After so many months of planning, it almost didn't seem real. There I was, with all the gear I carefully selected strapped to my back, hiking along in the sunshine, with more than 2,000 miles of trail ahead of me.

The trail in Georgia turned out to be very well maintained, and while it frequently went up and down in elevation, the hiking was not as rough as I expected. The AT is marked with white vertical bars that are painted on trees at eye level. The white bars, called blazes, are 2″ by 6″ and are reapplied often. The blazes are placed frequently enough that there is no question about whether or not you are walking on the proper trail. Other side trails are marked with blue or yellow blazes or different shaped markers so there is no confusion. The only way to get "lost" on the trail is to hike in the wrong direction without realizing it. I heard stories of this happening, but I never met anyone who had problems remembering which way to hike coming out of camp in the morning.

I quickly covered the seven miles and arrived at the Hawk Mountain shelter well before lunchtime. There were other hikers there, and like a pro, I sat down and ate my first lunch on the AT in the shelter. While eating, I thumbed through the *Data Book* and noticed that the next shelter, Gooch Gap shelter, was nine miles away. I considered my plan to limit my mileage in the beginning, but with almost a full day still ahead of me, I decided to nibble off a few more miles.

At Gooch Gap shelter I found a whole new set of hikers including six ladies from Indianapolis. Two of the six planned to hike the entire trail. The other four planned to leave the trail after a couple of weeks. We all cooked dinner, talked about gear, and of course talked about the trail. After dinner I set up my hammock, washed my pot (my only dish), and my fork (my only utensil), and then hung my food on the bear cable.

Bear cables were located about 50–100 feet away from the shelters in Georgia. They provided a convenient way to hang your food to discourage unwanted visitors during the night. The idea is to make all food inaccessible to the bears so they don't hang around the shelters. Bears that successfully find food around the shelters and campsites, become repeat visitors and usually turn into a nuisance. Problematic bears are often relocated by the park service to less populated areas. So really, the bear cables are constructed to protect the bears from us as well as to protect us from the bears.

Bear cables were new to me, but it didn't take long to figure out how they work. There are usually two or three pulleys attached to a horizontal cable, stretched between two trees about 30 feet high. Each pulley has another steel cable threaded through it that you use to hoist a small sack or "food bag" (which contains not only your food, but your stove, cooking pot and anything else that might smell like food) into the air. At a busy shelter there might be up to 10 food bags on one pulley.

Blood Mountain Shelter, just before Neels Gap. ▶

NEELS GAP

I can't believe the weather, it can only get worse. I got an early start this morning (started hiking at 7:30) and only planned to hike 11 miles to Woods Hole like most everyone planned to do who stayed at Gooch Gap with me last night. I reached Woods Hole a little after noon. After filling up my water containers from a nearby spring, and flipping through the Data Book, I decided to continue on another five miles to the hostel at Neels Gap where I am now.

I ended up breaking the day into three parts, eating lunches between them. I spent my first lunch break with two good looking girls who are also hiking to Maine.

The last section was up and down Blood Mountain, which was kind of difficult since I hiked it at the end of the day. Worse was the wicked sunburn I got on the back of my neck and arms. I really should have brought sun block along.

I like Neels Gap. I'm sleeping in the hostel, which comes with a free shower. Very deluxe. I had a few microwave pita pocket sandwiches and ice cream for dinner. Not the best, but it stretches my food out a bit.

The options for tomorrow are hiking 11 or 18 miles. I'll probably take it easy, but so far the going has been easy.

I hadn't really planned on getting to Neels Gap so quickly, but I felt so good hiking each day that I pushed on a little further than I planned. Although my actions didn't reflect it, I was nervous about hiking too many miles in the beginning. I felt great, but didn't want to injure myself. In the months leading up to my departure, I read many online journals from people who started thru-hiking and ended up leaving the trail because of a knee or foot injury. On the other hand, I felt I had to make progress toward Maine. Every day I was torn by how much mileage to do. I wanted to save my feet and legs, but I also wanted to click off miles on my trip. My obsession with "making miles" would define much of my hike.

The first outfitter along the AT is located at Neels Gap, only 31 miles from Springer Mountain. Before leaving for the trail, I identified Neels Gap as a key point. I looked at the first 31 miles as if they were a single backpacking trip. I felt secure knowing that if things went horribly wrong during the first few days with my gear or my attitude, I would pass by an outfitter early on and could make adjustments or pick up anything I forgot. It would be my second chance, so to speak, and 31 miles didn't seem as daunting at the start as 2,000 miles.

When I reached Neels Gap, all was well. I hadn't forgotten anything, my gear was working well and I had plenty of food. I was pleased with my planning.

There was a whole new set of hikers that I hadn't met before staying in the bunkhouse at Neels Gap. Another hiker mentioned that he was doing laundry and asked if I planned on washing my stuff. We combined loads and the washer was still only about half full. My laundry buddy hiked the AT the year before and made a face when I told him I hiked 16 miles that day. He told me what I already knew, that people usually take it easy the first couple of weeks so that they don't end up getting injured. I promised myself that the next day I would only hike the 11 or 12 miles to the next shelter.

Note in one of the laundry facilities along the trail

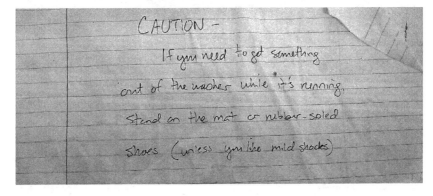

18

SNORING HIKERS

Neels Gap Hostel was packed last night, only one bunk was free. There was a lot of snoring and farting going on during the night in the bunkhouse. Nice.

It looks like rain today. Everyone here is planning to hike to Low Gap shelter tonight, which might be crowded. I'm going to hang out at Neels Gap for a while and have them weigh and go through my pack to help me lighten it up if possible. Last night some kid went from 52 to 33 pounds with the help of the storeowner.

There's a Golden Retriever here who is hiking the trail with his owner. He's even carrying his own little pack.

While preparing for my hike, I purchased a complete set of trail maps. I packed the first few maps before leaving for Georgia and planned to mail them home as I finished with them to save weight. I also made arrangements for my parents to mail me a new stock of maps at several key points along the trail.

At Neels Gap, I reassessed this strategy. The guys working at the outfitter helped me realize that I had only looked at one map one time, and it was clear I really didn't need any maps after all. I decided to send all of them home and asked my parents not to send any in the future. I also mailed home several sections of the *Companion* that I wouldn't need for months and some extra water purification items that I really didn't need.

I stayed at Neels Gap until 10:00 a.m., and then hiked on to Low Gap where I met up with several hikers I ran into earlier. The dog I saw with his pack, Barley, was sacked out in front of the shelter when I arrived, but woke up when two guys strolled in after dinner with another dog. The two guys looked like they were probably on a section hike and were pretty scary looking. If I had been at the shelter alone when they arrived, I probably would have broken camp and left. As it was, I managed to keep my promise to myself of hiking low miles and stayed put at Low Gap.

The evening dragged on while most of us sat around a picnic table making small talk about hiking gear. After dinner I set up my hammock, washed my pot and fork, and hung my food on the bear cable. My simple routine was beginning to develop.

SASSAFRAS GAP

It is day five and I'm still in Georgia as expected. Everything around here seems to be called Sassafras this or Sassafras that. Tonight I'm staying at one of the Sassafras Gaps.

The morning started out poorly. It was raining when I woke up, so I packed up without eating and started out early. The rain got heavier and soon thunder joined in. Keep in mind that the AT follows ridges and when possible, goes over mountaintops.

At one point I stopped for half an hour to let the storm pass, which meant I ended up standing around getting cold. When the storm moved off into the distance, I began hiking again, which warmed me up despite the continuing rain.

After hiking for about three hours, the deluge eased up and the sky brightened. After another half hour the sun was blazing. Things were looking up.

I heard from a passing hiker that someone was serving breakfast at Unicorn Gap, but when I arrived, the rumored meal wasn't there. So I lightened my food bag of some crackers and peanut butter. Soon after, I started feeling sick to my stomach. For the past few days I've had an upset stomach, but I'm not sure why. Maybe I'm eating too much peanut butter.

Lunch was courtesy of a Boy Scout troop. The troop sets up camp near Trey Mountain every year around this time and for several days they cook breakfast, lunch and dinner for passing thru-hikers.

When I arrived, the scouts had a huge spread of food. Everything a hungry thru-hiker might want, including hamburgers, hotdogs and all the condiments. There were many other hikers eating and the grill was going non-stop. One of the adults with the troop, possibly the scoutmaster, pulled out a guitar and played a few songs.

There is such a thing as a free lunch after all.

While hiking, I sometimes encountered what is known as "trail magic." Trail magic takes many forms. Sometimes I'd stumble upon a stream full of cold sodas on a hot day, or perhaps, after the fifth meal in a row of Ramen noodles, I'd unexpectedly find someone grilling burgers on the side of the trail. Trail magic could even be as simple as an offering of a spare candy bar from a day hiker.

Early on, when my appetite was adjusting to life on the trail, I could almost rely on trail magic. It was common for people to set up their magic where the trail crossed a road. This was especially true on weekends. After a while, the sound of rushing cars would make me salivate.

I was conflicted. While the frequent offerings of trail magic took some of the magic out of it and made the trail seem less wild, I was always hungry and every bit of it made me immensely happy.

For most of the first week of my trip, the weather was perfect. Sunny days, low humidity and cool temperatures put me off to a great start. I enjoyed the natural setting I hiked through every day. It was still early spring and in the mountains the leaves were not yet out on the trees. Occasionally, the trail would dip down to lower elevations where the leaves were just beginning to emerge. I savored those first days and wondered if I'd have good weather for the whole trip. I didn't. The following months brought record setting rains to the East Coast.

▲ *Taking a break on Blood Mountain*
◄ *Trail magic*

The first state line.

One State Down

THERE IS NO SHORTAGE OF HIKERS on the AT in April. During the day the trail didn't seem very crowded since most people were hiking northbound and there wasn't much two-way traffic, but at night the shelters and campsites were packed with hikers. While in Georgia, I seemed to hike just a bit farther than most people each day, which meant that I camped with different people each night. I'm shy by nature, and this made it hard for me to get to know people. I hiked through Georgia without a trail name and continued to introduce myself to other thru-hikers as just "Andy."

Georgia was behind me. Except for one rainy morning, the weather was perfect. I noticed that for some reason the trees in Georgia didn't have any buds showing yet. I finally saw some just before the North Carolina border.

North Carolina didn't look so good weather-wise. A couple of hikers who had recently taken a break in a nearby town said that the weather forecast was for cold temperatures and rain.

It was raining lightly when I arrived at Muskrat Creek shelter. One thing I noticed that was different from the shelters in Georgia was that it didn't have bear cables. I guessed they didn't have a bear problem yet.

My hammock's flexibility proved useful, as all of the tent pads, even the less desirable ones, were already taken. During my last couple of days in Georgia, I read in the shelter registers about a large herd of hikers that were traveling together up the trail. I caught part of that herd. I set up my hammock next to a creek and settled in.

HELLO NORTH CAROLINA

The weekends continue to be good for free food. Yesterday, around lunchtime, I walked up on a man who was grilling hot dogs by the side of the trail. He asked if I wanted some. It turned out that he thru-hiked the AT in 2000, and now comes out a couple of times a year to cook for thru-hikers.

Red from Rochester, a hiker named Brian and Brian's girlfriend were also there eating. I saw them the day before when we all enjoyed the Boy Scout troop burgers and ended up camping with them at Sassafras Gap. After lunch, the three of them walked to a nearby town to take it easy, but I continued hiking.

After hiking 76 miles in 6 days, I crossed my first state line. The border was marked with a small piece of wood nailed to a tree. I set my gear down and took the obligatory state line photo.

Within minutes of arriving in North Carolina, the weather began to change. The wind picked up and the skies darkened — it was almost as if the state line was an invisible boundary that the foul weather obeyed. To make things more dramatic, the trail widened into a grassy area that contained an old twisted, gnarled tree. The tree looked spooky under the dark sky.

I was only planning on hiking to the state line today, but I pushed on three more miles to the Muskrat Creek shelter where I am right now. The shelter is packed with hikers. This is by far the most crowded shelter I've seen.

I didn't have a second lunch today, which I've become accustomed to eating, and I'm paying for it now. I ate a decent dinner, but my stomach is feeling a little sick again. I plan to take it easy for the next few days. My legs and feet feel great, but they could probably use some shorter days.

It rained hard during the night and I wondered if I would wake up over the creek rather than next to it. I faired well though, and was happy to be snug in my hammock when I saw that many people's tents had flooded during the night, soaking their gear.

Before I started hiking the AT, I decided not to camp inside the shelters. This decision was mostly based on the fact that I had read that you could not count on getting a spot in one every night. After a week on the trail, I had seen many shelters and had sat inside them while snacking or eating lunch during the day, but I had not slept in one. I became curious about what I might be missing by sleeping outside in my hammock, so I decided to try sleeping inside one for a change. The Muskrat Creek shelter was too crowded to make my shelter debut, so the next day I decided to stop hiking a little early and secure a spot in the shelter at Carter Gap.

It turned out that one night in a shelter was enough to turn me off to them for months. Since the shelters were crowded, the real estate you claim for the night was defined by the width of your sleeping bag, which meant that you slept with people packed in on either side of you. Aside from being uncomfortable, the mice came out at night. To keep the mice from eating holes in my pack, I hung it up from the ceiling on a string. Most shelters have strings already hung for this purpose and most have an old tuna can placed midway down so the mice have a difficult time sliding down the string to your pack. Of course, this meant that the mice just ran around the floor where I slept.

During the night, I heard the mice, but I didn't really have any problems with them. It was common to hear stories about mice running over people's faces during the night, but experienced hikers who frequented the shelters (also known as "shelter rats"), knew to sleep with a little room between their head and the back wall of the shelter to give the mice an alternate route to running over their face. After one night in a shelter, I couldn't see the attraction.

My plan from the beginning was to do the trail in style. If there was an option to get the deluxe version of something, I planned to get it. This plan lasted just over a week. At the Rainbow Springs campground in North Carolina, I had an opportunity to stay under a real roof. The campground offered a bunkhouse and cabins. Without hesitation, I rented a cabin.

While I was inside my cabin drying my gear out, showering in my own shower, and cooking a pizza in my own oven, almost everyone else was in the bunkhouse. I ended up gravitating to the bunkhouse and spent most of the evening on the porch there hanging out with other hikers. From that point on, when I got off the trail to spend the night at a campground or in a town, I stayed where everyone else stayed, which usually meant cheap hotels and even cheaper hostels.

IN A FOG

Today I got a late start. I was ready for the 9:00 a.m. shuttle back to the trail from the Rainbow Springs campground, but it was clear that the driver wouldn't be leaving at 9:00. I figured it was worth waiting, since the alternative was to hike uphill a mile to the point where I left the trail.

The shuttle was "about to leave" for over an hour. Finally, Blaze, Pipes, Windtalker and I were in the truck and on our way. The other hikers were all about 10 years younger than me and in their early 20s.

Blaze got a mohawk before starting the trail and painted it white so it would look like the blazes marking the AT. He didn't use hair dye or paint though; it looks like he used the same white tar that is used to paint lines on a highway.

Pipes works at Eastern Mountain Sports back in the real world. Right now she is lugging around a 40+ pound pack, but she doesn't seem to mind.

Windtalker ordered a lightweight tent months ago, but hasn't received it. So she leaves a voicemail message for the guy who makes the tent every chance she has, in hopes that he can deliver it to her somewhere along the AT. For now, she's sleeping under a borrowed tarp.

As we left the campground, it looked like it would be a clear day for the first time in North Carolina, but it was a trick. On the drive up the mountain back to the trail, we ascended into the cloud that has covered the trail since I left Georgia.

It was 11:00 a.m. when I finally got back on the trail. The woods were engulfed in fog and everything felt and smelled damp. The rain held off, but the views were hidden in the clouds. So although the hiking was good, there wasn't much to see along the way. I had planned a big mileage day to reach the Nantahala Outdoor Center (NOC), but with the late start, that wasn't going to happen.

I usually camp near a shelter, but tonight about 10 of us are camping near Wayah Bald. It's only 7:00 p.m., but everyone is snug in their tents, with the exception of Windtalker, who is sleeping under her tarp.

FIRST TRACKS

Overnight, the rain turned to sleet. Still in the clouds, condensation is a problem and it ended up raining inside my hammock.

I woke up early to reach NOC before the post office there closed. While I was eating breakfast, the sleet turned to snow. The trail was pretty slippery most of the way, but my legs and feet felt good all day, so it wasn't really a problem.

The trail has been completely fogged in since I entered North Carolina, so I'm missing most of the views, but it's still very enjoyable being out in nature everyday. Occasionally, I'll round a bend in the trail and stop and listen for a bit. Sometimes I'll hear animals walking through the underbrush, or hear a bird call. I know, it doesn't sound very exciting. I guess you have to be here to understand.

I received an email from a friend asking, "What do you think about while hiking all day?" Truthfully, not much. I think about other people I've met on the trail, when I'll be able to refill my water and if there will be any bunks left at NOC when I arrive. I also wonder if I am hiking too many miles each day and if I should take a zero day (a day when you don't hike). I don't actually resolve anything, I just think. Many times I'm zoned out while I hike, and just relax.

I arrived at NOC around 1:00 p.m. The hiking was pretty flat, except the last five miles, which were down a steep slippery hill. Right now I'm washing every stitch of clothing I have with me, which means I'm standing here freezing in the laundry room in just my rain suit. When I'm off the trail, my chores are laundry, showering and eating huge quantities of food.

Snow visited the trail

NOC was a milestone for me. It is located right on the trail, and I had selected it for my first mail-drop. Friends of mine, Pete and Michaela, volunteered to mail me food and supplies while I was on the trail. This is a popular re-supply technique. Through them, I had the best support of any hiker on the trail. I would email them a shopping list and the name of a business along the AT that would hold my mail, and when I arrived a few days later, my order would be waiting. It usually included a picture from home, a note and even special homemade goodies.

My mail-drop was waiting at NOC and included oatmeal chocolate chip cookies! The new food supply weighed more than my pack though, so I was a little concerned about how I would carry it all.

NOC is all about kayaking, canoeing and rafting. They have tons of great things to do and the Nantahala River runs right through it. I thought it would be a great place to visit after finishing my hike.

The toll the miles were taking on some hikers began to show, and NOC resembled a hospital ward. A few really bad cases hobbled around so slowly that I wondered how they even hiked the last miles into NOC. Most "patients" were planning to spend a few days there to rest their legs, while others were waiting for a ride home. This got me thinking about my own legs and how to keep them healthy.

Normally I don't see other hikers more than one night at a time on the trail, but Windtalker was at the last few campsites with me, and I slowly got to know her. I have a hard time starting conversations with strangers, but Windtalker was very outgoing and easy to talk to. At NOC, she persuaded me to join her, Pipes and Iron Chef Connecticut in taking a zero day. I felt great and didn't really think I needed to take a day off the trail, yet everyone I talked to had already taken at least one zero day. I felt lazy even considering it.

Me and Pipes rafting at NOC

Flirting With Hypothermia

O N MY FIRST ZERO DAY, Windtalker, Pipes, Iron Chef Connecticut and I went whitewater rafting. Now, if I had driven to NOC to go rafting that day, I think I would have bagged it. The forecast was for snow and the Nantahala River was still very cold. But, hiking in for one day only and knowing we'd have a warm place to sleep at night put a different slant on things. Besides, NOC rented wetsuits so we felt that we'd be fine.

We rented our gear and took a shuttle bus up-river. The plan was to ride in two, two-person ducky rafts back downstream to NOC. Windtalker and Iron Chef Connecticut piled into one raft, and Pipes and I climbed into the other.

The river was pretty tame, but still wild enough to get soaked. It started out great, but after a couple of hours, we got cold — very cold. In fact, I've honestly never been so cold in my life. My entire body was shivering, bordering on convulsing. I knew NOC wasn't too far away, and that I wasn't in any real danger, but somewhere down the river I became so frozen that I lost control of my hands. About that time, we met the largest section of rapids.

Pipes and I were in front of Windtalker and Iron Chef Connecticut, so we headed into the churning water first. In an instant, our boat flipped belly-up and we were thrown into the water. I surfaced right under the raft, which must have been bobbing in a hydraulic. Before I could panic, I was spit out down river. I looked around for Pipes, and as soon as she surfaced, rescue lines were tossed out to us. It turned out we were right by NOC and their guides were ready to help us. There was just one problem. My hands were so cold that I couldn't grab onto the rescue rope. I wrapped the rope around my arm, but I continued slipping down it. Things weren't looking so good, but there weren't any rapids immediately downstream. As I reached the end of the rope, I found a wooden disc that was tied to the end and managed to hold onto that.

Windtalker and Iron Chef Connecticut went through the rapids next. Their raft flipped in the same hydraulic and more rescue lines went out. We walked the short distance into NOC and were greeted with hot showers and warm food. We spent the rest of the day lounging around eating and relaxing. I was truly on vacation.

Windtalker, Pipes and Iron Chef Connecticut were a lot of fun. I didn't know Iron Chef Connecticut previously, and he turned out to be an interesting guy. He prepared and dehydrated all his meals for his AT hike before he left — which is a major undertaking. Thanks to these three, my first experience doing something off the trail with hikers turned out to be a good one.

BACK ON THE TRAIL

Before we left NOC, we had a pack lightening party. Basically, everyone dumped out their packs and decided what to send home, bounce (by mail) to the next town or throw away. Very exciting stuff. After mailing out the gear that didn't make the cut, we headed back to the trail. The weather finally cleared up and there is now more than 100 feet of visibility from the vistas.

The zero day worked like magic and my feet and legs felt like butter all day, although I only hiked eight miles. I do have a new problem, however. I aggravated my shoulder rafting yesterday and it hurt pretty badly all day. I'm not sure how it will heal while I'm carrying a pack, but I guess time will tell.

Most of the snow melted during the day today, but a snowman greeted Windtalker and me at Cheoah Bald. We decided to camp since the views were excellent. When Pipes and Iron Chef Connecticut hiked up, we easily convinced them to camp with us. The bald is a very neat place to spend the night. It's the highest point around and since there are few trees, we have a nice view of a neighboring ridge.

Shortly after we set up camp, Play came along and joined us. He then proceeded to collect firewood by climbing whatever trees he could find and breaking off dead limbs. The kid is nuts. For dinner he ate peanut butter straight from the jar with loads of honey mixed in. That definitely would have given me an upset stomach.

We all relaxed on the side of a hill as more and more people streamed in. We ate, watched the sun set and then watched Play tend to the fire. Things are much more relaxed around camp when the weather is nice.

After 11 days on the trail, I still do not have a trail name. I'm "just Andy." The rafters are the first people I've had any kind of relationship with, so they feel they have to name me. Windtalker does adventure races and has an iron distance triathlon on her agenda. Iron Chef Connecticut and Pipes are both considering running a marathon. So it came up in conversation that I've done an Ironman®. So the rafting crew is now calling me "Ironman." I think I'm going to pass on the name though — it just doesn't feel right.

Pipes and Windtalker at NOC going through their mail drops.

The next morning, the topic of my trail name came up again. Since I rejected their first name, Ironman, someone came up with "Iron Toothpick."

I don't really think of myself as being skinny, and initially took offense to the "Toothpick" part of the name. But the reality is that I am skinny, really skinny, and was even more so while hiking the AT. After a few hours the name started to sink in.

My obsession with mileage was beginning to emerge. I liked hanging out with the rafters, but between the zero day and the short eight mile day to Cheoah Bald, I felt that I had to get moving. While the rafters were still in their sleeping bags, I packed up my stuff, let them know I was going to Fontana Dam and left. I knew this was further than any of them planned to hike. They all had packages waiting for them at the post office in Fontana Dam, but since it was Sunday, the post office was closed and there was no reason for them to rush.

FONTANA DAM

A few things came together today to put me in a bad mood. My shoulder is killing me, I'm not eating enough, and I realized I don't have enough food to get through the Smoky Mountains. The good news is that my feet and legs are as good as ever. I'm sure most people out here would gladly trade my problems for their foot/leg pain.

The trail comes out of the woods in a back corner of the parking lot to a marina at Fontana Dam. The dam forms a lake, which you can see from about 12 miles away on the AT, so for hours you think you are almost there.

In the parking lot is an information board and a telephone that connects to a 24-hour shuttle service. Pretty cool. The shuttle takes you to Fontana Village, which was originally built to house people working on the dam. Now, it is a resort and the super-friendly staff goes out of their way to make hikers feel comfortable. This improved my mood, and I decided to stay here tonight.

Madonna and Sweet Ass were already here (I briefly met them before while camping one night). Madonna is a physical therapist and often sings around camp. Not just the usual camp singing, but really good singing. Sweet Ass is a guy about my age who has a seasoned look and a military background.

We all went to dinner together with some other hikers who are staying here too. After watching an episode of the Simpsons, we played pool, which probably wasn't the best thing to do for my sore shoulder.

Right now it's late and the pain from my shoulder is keeping me awake. The resort, while nice, just opened for the season and the ice machine isn't on, so there's no ice for my shoulder. As I lay here, I'm debating what to do about my situation. The weather forecast is good, so I don't want to stay here and blow a good week of weather trying to heal my shoulder. I guess it will probably hurt no matter where I am, so I'll probably press on.

Fontana Dam

I used to swim a lot, and one summer I strained both my shoulders while completing a four-mile swim across the Chesapeake Bay in Maryland. I chose to ignore the pain though and continued to swim a few times a week in the following months. The pain slowly got worse.

Finally, one day, while cutting a couple of 2×4s to fit into my car in The Home Depot parking lot, my right shoulder went. The pain was excruciating, but I gutted out the rest of the cut and brought my lumber home. Within hours, the pain became unbearable. It was intense pain like I had never felt before and it lasted for days. After visiting a doctor, I found out that I had a mostly torn rotator cuff and just narrowly avoided surgery. With a break from swimming, and some occasional physical therapy, my shoulder healed almost 100 percent. Almost. Although I didn't feel anything unusual during the rafting trip, I must have aggravated my rotator cuff again.

INTO THE SMOKIES

I got a late start out of Fontana Village. I bought more food, checked out the dam, read the obligatory information about the history of the dam, then set out.

Around noon, I entered Great Smoky Mountains National Park. It was hot out and there I was climbing into the mountains with a throbbing shoulder, weighed down by a week's worth of food. Ten miles into the park, I stopped at a shelter. I was worn out and a bit depressed since I was hiking slower than normal.

I cooked some pasta which made me feel better right away. After resting for about half an hour, I decided to push on. The next shelter was only two miles away, and I knew I would feel better about my day if I nipped off those two miles.

The ground leveled off and what a difference it made. I felt great — like I could walk to Maine non-stop. When I arrived at the shelter, some other hikers already had a fire going. Life is good again.

Sunset on Cheoah Bald.

I remember how difficult it was to deal with the pain in the comfort of my home, and I wasn't sure how I could do it on the trail. For a few days, I worried that my shoulder might end my hike, but finally I decided that my shoulder was not critical to hiking. I might as well cover some miles while it healed and just do my best to avoid further aggravating it.

The only bad part about this decision was that I was about to enter the Smoky Mountains, where a week-long stretch of trail awaited with only a single road crossing. If my shoulder got any worse, it would be difficult to leave the trail quickly.

Unfortunately, my shoulder pain was really getting me down. Already, I was looking forward to taking another relaxing zero day in Hot Springs in about a week. I hoped to be able to get some ice there and give my shoulder proper attention. One good thing I noticed was that my shoulder tolerated sleeping in my hammock much better than sleeping in the bed at Fontana Village. I think this was because the hammock curled up around it and provided some support.

After a mostly unpleasant first day in the Smokies, I went to bed thinking about what went wrong and what I could do to avoid another unhappy day. Before drifting off, I decided to nap during the hottest part of the day. While this wouldn't help my shoulder any, at least I would avoid the unpleasantness of the heat.

I got an early start the next day and ended up hiking with Pez in the morning. He's a cool guy that other hikers had told me about, but I hadn't met him before. We hiked together for a bit and exchanged the typical trail small talk about gear, trail conditions and where we planned to spend the night.

One thing I discovered was that hiking actually distracted me from my shoulder pain. I hiked 10 miles, then executed the nap phase of my new plan. Napping in my hammock on a nice day in the Smokies wasn't too bad. While I hung out napping (literally), a few people stopped nearby for lunch. I wondered what they thought about the guy sacked out in the middle of the day in his hammock.

TAX DAY

Tonight I'm staying at the Double Spring Gap shelter (actually, outside the shelter in my hammock as usual), about a mile away from Clingman's Dome, the highest point on the AT.

Double Spring is named for two unreliable springs about 150 feet apart. One is in North Carolina and the other is in Tennessee.

I saw a lot of hikers today. Many people park at Clingman's Dome and do various day hikes from there. I met a couple from McLean, Virginia (near where I live) who were down here for a few days.

Tomorrow my hiking options are either 13 or 20 miles. I think my preference is for 17-mile days, so I'm in a quandary. These are my problems nowadays. Last year at this time I was doing my taxes.

Tonight a group of us were talking about the thru-hiker dropout rate. Someone said that only 15 percent of the people who start the AT finish. One fifth apparently drop out within the first 30 miles. So, as hikers that made it this far, we figured we each had a one in three chance of finishing. This means that of the nine thru-hikers around the fire tonight, only three of us will make it. This floored me. I looked around and all of the people here looked like they had what it takes. It was odd thinking that a few of them (or possibly me) might not make it to Maine.

Pez. I would see Pez on and off from the Smokies through Pennsylvania.

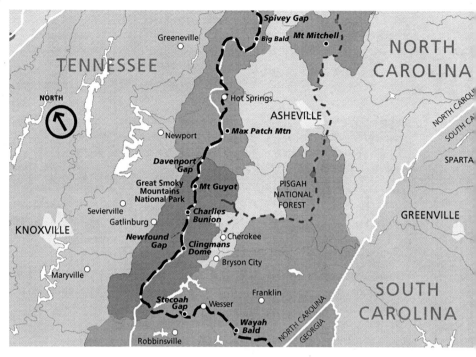

For the first time since beginning my hike, I looked around and sized up the other thru-hikers. I'd been hiking with most of them on and off for days and nobody was complaining about any injuries (well, except for me with my shoulder). Everyone seemed competent enough; I found it hard to believe that anyone in the group wouldn't finish.

The statistic taunts. Less than five months later, I found out it held true. Of the folks around the campfire that night, only three of us finished the trail. I still can't believe it.

I want to talk to the people who left the trail and find out what happened. I want to find out what kind of issues made them quit. But once they quit, you don't see them anymore so you never find out.

The definition of a thru-hike is purposefully vague, but most seem to define it as hiking every bit of the trail in one year. Some folks set out to hike the whole trail, but do not want to take off five or six months of work at one time. These people are called section hikers and they hike a little bit of the trail each year. After a few years, or a few decades in some cases, they complete the trail.

Occasionally, you meet a section hiker who started their first section hike as a thru-hiker. Bad luck turned their thru-hike into a section hike and they return to the AT to finish the remaining portion another year. They all have different stories and they all, without exception, regret their decision to leave the trail. It's a distorted survey of course, since I only spoke with people whose desire to complete the AT was strong enough to bring them back.

One such person was a section hiker I walked with for a few days. I'll call him James, not because I think he would be embarrassed, but because when I was hiking I was not planning to write a book and never asked for permission to share his story.

James was a thin older man with gray hair and a matching gray beard. He was thin, but not toothpick thin like me. In another lifetime, he lived in my hometown, Reston, Virginia. A few years ago, he started a thru-hike. Midway through his hike, he developed foot pain. By the time he reached Kent, Connecticut, the pain became so unbearable that he made the decision to leave the AT.

He said it was a hard decision, one of the hardest of his life. In Kent he called his wife and told her he was coming home. He said he cried on the bus-ride the whole way back. It must have been a lonely ride. All of the hikers he had met were continuing on, having a good time, and he didn't even have a chance to say goodbye or let them know he was leaving.

Well, James was back, looked good and most likely finished his second section. After talking to James I am sure that he got much more out of his hike than I did.

The people who really fascinate me are those who just stop for no apparent reason. I'm not sure why I find these people so interesting. Part of me wonders if it is possible to just suddenly feel so down that you have no control over the decision to quit. You just find yourself on a bus home one day and wonder what happened. I was afraid it would happen to me. Afraid that one day I'd wake up, happen to be in a town with a bus station and decide to take the bus out of town instead of the trail.

The hikers I met from McLean, Virginia while at Double Spring Gap shelter, were headed home the following day. Through them I felt close to home and I also felt that if needed, they could give me a ride home. I never considered if they would actually want to give me a ride. At the time I was in full-blown thru-hiker mode and just assumed they would be honored.

Standing Bear Hostel, just north of the Smokies.

LONG DAYS

My shoulder pain is beginning to fade. I think my hammock not only provides relief, but actually helps take the pain away by taking the pressure off just the right part of it. In any case, it's slowly feeling better, so I've stopped worrying about it and am devoting all my attention to obsessing about my mileage.

I put in two 20+ mile days in a row, and I am now staying at Standing Bear Hostel. The hostel is a group of buildings that a man named Curtis and his girlfriend built behind their house. It's a good hiker compound, they even sell supplies. There's a barbeque pit, a covered eating area and a bunkhouse. There's even an old laptop for dialing into the Internet. One of the cabins, the deluxe cabin, is built over a creek.

I came in late and ended up sleeping in a top bunk without a mattress. People with tents carry sleeping mats, but people in hammocks, like me, go without one to save weight. So my mattress is plywood. Ugh.

Standing Bear Hostel wasn't in my plan for tonight, but a day hiker I ran into from around here recommended it, so I thought I'd check it out. It's no Fontana Village, but it has its own cool vibe.

The hostel's clothes washer is broken, so I'm in Curtis' house right now, in my rain suit, waiting for my laundry to dry.

My hike yesterday went well. The trail was shady and the leaves are starting to come out more. I ran into Pez and Blaze again. They night hiked together from 1:15 a.m. to 6:15 a.m. The section they hiked was overgrown, with a lot of warnings about bears. I would have been totally spooked out.

Last night I stayed at Pecks shelter. Everyone thought it would rain so we all slept in the shelter for once (in the Smokies you are required to sleep in the shelters because of bears, although it seems that most people choose to camp outside anyway). I managed to get some decent sleep despite being in a shelter.

Today ended up being a 23-mile day. I felt good until I slipped and fell on a slimy rock while crossing a stream. I tested my waterproofing and tweaked my shoulder a bit as I lay turtled in a pool of freezing cold water. For a moment, I thought I had serious problems, but I managed to pull myself out of the water. Now, hours later, I feel fine and my PocketMail and camera escaped injury.

So things are good after two long days in a row. I now have to decide if I should do a third long day to put myself in position to get to the Hot Springs post office before it closes at noon on Saturday (which is the day after tomorrow). Two friends threatened by email to send me packages, and I don't want to wait until Monday for homemade cookies.

Life is pretty complicated on the trail.

Just the facts

The rafters are greeted by a snowman

I lucked out with the weather in the Smoky Mountains, with warm temperatures and clear skies the whole way through. There were still remnants of the snow that fell the week before, but that was quickly disappearing.

I became part of a loose group of hikers. The primary thing we had in common was that we all hiked about the same distance every day and congregated around the same shelters in the evening. Other than that, the group was diverse.

One hiker was a professional first mate on ocean-going yachts. He told us about sailing in the Mediterranean, rich clients, and modern day pirates that carry equally modern assault rifles. He was between assignments and was hiking the AT until his next job came through.

I saw two of the other hikers, George and Hoser, my first night in North Carolina. They were both in their mid-twenties. George looked like he was just too cool to be around, like someone who reads the news on MTV®. He turned out to be okay though.

Hoser was from Michigan, and George was from Ohio. Apparently, there is some rivalry between the two and sometimes, around the campfire, they put on the Hoser & George Show. It started out with a few simple questions like: "How many Buckeyes does it take to screw in a light bulb," or "Did you hear about the girl from Michigan who . . ." At some point they both sang school fight songs.

Another hiker I consistently saw was an older man from Pennsylvania who was on his third thru-hike in as many years. He was a wealth of information and answered everyone's questions about what was ahead on the trail. It was from this man that I received my first warning about the difficult terrain in the White Mountains of New Hampshire.

Another member of our loosely defined group was Wild Flamingo. Wild Flamingo was a retired truck driver from Florida. When he was a teenager, he worked at a grocery store. As soon as it was legal for him to do so, he drove the store's truck. After 20 years of truck driving (mostly big rigs), he retired at age 36 and was roaming the earth. Wild Flamingo got his name because his handle during his truck driving days was Flamingo. He would sometimes catch up to the group for a few days and then disappear for a week before I'd see him again. Wild Flamingo's reappearance usually coincided with trips into towns that had all you can eat buffets. He was thin, but could consume huge quantities of food.

Happy, another hiker I saw frequently, was from Colorado and mentioned he was an Olympic athlete of some sort. Happy was quiet and really didn't smile much, so I'm not sure how he got his trail name. He looked rough, like he would be comfortable in a fight-to-the-death cage match.

NIGHT HIKING

Yesterday (Friday), my focus was to make sure I reached Hot Springs before the post office closed on Saturday (today). There are various rumors that on Saturdays it closes either at 10:30 a.m., or at noon. Missing the post office would mean that I would spend my zero day without my mail-drop (and without my cookies). I thought about how far to walk and how early I could get myself up this morning to rush into town.

The terrain was easy, but after two of my longest days yet, I was glad to stop after 18 miles. The problem was that 15 miles still remained between me and Hot Springs. Feeling achy, I resigned myself to getting my mail-drop on Monday. Fifteen miles was just too much to do before 10:30 a.m.

After dinner, Gorilla, Yogibear and Happy showed up and said they planned to night hike another five miles. Going another five miles would mean that I would only need to hike 10 miles in the morning. That might make it possible to reach the post office before it closed. I decided to join them.

We all left, except for Yogibear, Gorilla's hiking partner, who was still finishing up dinner. Gorilla announced that we would hike out easy so that Yogibear could catch up. Five miles of the fastest hiking I've done on this trip followed. I know I'm not an Olympic athlete, but I also know the difference between easy and all out. We weren't going easy.

Soon after we left it got dark, so we turned on our headlights and kept moving. We covered five miles pretty quickly, but kept on going. I don't know what kind of relationship Gorilla and Yogibear have, but it involves one hiking as fast as he can so that the other has to hike alone, an unknown distance, in the dark.

More distance at night meant less distance in the morning, so I was fine with our adventure race. My legs felt surprisingly good until the last two miles. By then, I had overdone it for the day and split away from Gorilla and Happy. At 11:30 p.m., I arrived at the last shelter before Hot Springs, just shortly after them.

Although I'm normally anti-shelter, late at night, after hiking a total of 30 miles in one day, I was really hoping for a shelter spot. I'm sure all three of us were thinking the same thing. The shelters have been packed though, so there was almost no chance of a single shelter spot, and certainly not three.

We quietly walked up to the shelter to scope it out. It was empty — unbelievable. It was the first empty shelter I've seen. I wasn't sure whether I should be happy or spooked. I chose happy.

I began laying my stuff out on the shelter floor when I heard growling. I looked up to a frozen Gorilla and Happy. They were both fixed on something in the darkness I couldn't see. I quickly went from happy to scared.

It turned out that people were in tents near the shelter and one of those tents housed four Great Danes, two of them full grown. Talk about cozy. Now, in daylight, a Great Dane is just a big goofy dog. At midnight, in the middle of the woods, a pair of growling Great Danes can really get your heart rate going.

As it turns out, I followed my two longest days with a 30-mile day. Probably not the best thing for my legs, but I have a zero day coming up.

Yogibear never showed up at the shelter.

Big Bald on a cold and windy morning

Will Trail Run for Cookies

WHEN I WAS A KID, I walked a half mile to the school bus stop almost every morning. One day, I left the house a few minutes late. Worried that I would miss the bus, I decided to run. As a third grader, I knew that if I ran I would get to the bus stop quicker.

While I was running, I visualized success. I imagined seeing the school bus just as I was on the last stretch. I imagined that Mrs. Hodkins, the school bus driver, saw me just in time and waited for me.

With my backpack heavy with schoolbooks, I ran and ran. I finally came into the last stretch, but no school bus was waiting. I kept running until I was at the bus stop. There was no bus, no kids waiting for the bus — nothing. I had missed the bus. Now what?

Then I saw some friends walking toward me. It struck me as odd that they were so calm, considering that we all missed the bus. Then, slowly, my third grade mind put two and two together and realized that I was early, very early.

Any fourth grader knows that you only need to run a little bit if you are a little bit late.

In the morning I was still concerned about getting to the post office in Hot Springs before it closed. Despite hiking three long days in a row, I felt good, so I thought about running. My pack, lacking any food at that point, was light and the terrain was soft and flat, but more importantly, there were cookies waiting.

I was cautious that I might overdo things by running. As I walked, I thoughtfully surveyed the critical areas. My feet felt good, my ankles had never given me the slightest complaint, my knees were fine, even my shoulder — which gave me pain for days — seemed fine. With all systems "go," I was off for an early morning run. As I ran, I thought about that morning in the third grade when I was late for the bus.

Hot Springs is a true trail town. The white markers that are painted on trees (and on Blaze's head) go right down Main Street in the center of town. Hot Springs was just waking up as I ran in. There were a few things I looked for when stopping in a town: A good outfitter, a place to stay, a laundromat, a bar and cheap food. All of those things should be close together and as close to the trail as possible. In Hot Springs, those things are literally right on the AT.

Before shopping for groceries, I always had some idea of how much food I needed to carry with me to make it to the next re-supply point. I scanned the *Data Book* to find the next re-supply store that was close to the trail. Typically, I'd have to make some critical decisions, like whether I'd rather hike with three days of food and re-supply at a store located several miles off the trail, or hike with five days of food and re-supply at a store located just one mile from the trail.

After selecting my next re-supply point, I'd scan the book for places located reasonably close to the trail that offered meals. Knowing how many days I needed food for, minus any meals I could buy along the way, provided me with the information I needed to effectively grocery shop.

After shopping, I picked up my mail from the post office. I knew Hoser wasn't far behind me on the trail and that he had a mail-drop waiting for him as well, so I talked the postal employee into giving me his mail too. That way he wasn't without his Easter candy on Easter.

I found a place to stay and was settled in before noon. That left lots of time to eat food and rest.

Journal Entry
April 20

DOING NOTHING

Today was unexciting compared to my last zero day. No hypothermia or swimming in hydraulics.

The day consisted of eating, doing laundry, eating, napping, eating and more eating. The scale here says I've lost 15 pounds, so consuming calories is top priority.

Eating the cookies and Easter candy from my mail-drop all day should help me gain a few pounds. I was really jazzed to get not one but two care packages yesterday. I've bounced a few cookies ahead by mail to Damascus, in Virginia, since I couldn't eat everything in one day.

Of course, some of the goodies will leave town in my backpack.

Hoser started his hike with the gear he had in stock. He planned to check out what worked for other hikers and re-gear on the trail at some point. He decided that Hot Springs was the place. He completely re-geared from his pack to his shoes. It was a happy day for the outfitter.

After 20 days on the trail, George was still going by George. A few folks decided that he needed a trail name. George followed horse racing and suggested he be named after a famous horse, like Secretariat or Man of War. Hoser came back with "Mr. Ed." George wasn't too enthusiastic at first, but after a few days he warmed up to the name.

Hanging out in Hot Springs was like hanging out in a small town you grew up in. I instantly knew where everything was. With all of the hikers milling about, I also felt that I knew everyone, or at least had seen them before. For two days Hot Springs had an odd homey feeling to it.

After leaving Hot Springs, on the approach to my next state, Tennessee, I saw "300" written on the ground in rocks. After consulting the *Data Book,* it turned out I had hiked 300 miles.

A few days out of Hot Springs, the trail passed near Erwin, Tennessee. Erwin is the home of Miss Janet and a few people mentioned that Miss Janet's was a "don't miss" spot. I only planned on hiking the AT once, so I figured I would be a bit of a tourist and check out all of the "don't miss" places.

MISS JANET

Right now I'm at Miss Janet's house, in clothes that aren't mine, doing laundry. Everyone talks about how cool this place is on the trail. They don't mention that it is total confusion.

I showed up, found a bunk (which I later found out was someone else's bunk), showered, changed into spare clothes that Miss Janet keeps in stock, and started my laundry. I did all of this before meeting Miss Janet.

Miss Janet converted two of the downstairs rooms in her house into bunkrooms. The place is a total mess. Hikers, gear and a few dogs, some which are Miss Janet's, form a chaotic mix.

There is junk everywhere and nobody knows what is going on and everyone is okay with that. Miss Janet also has two teenage daughters. One guy has been here for a week, most likely because of one of the daughters.

This morning, I hiked over Big Bald, which was very windy. A combination of wind and humidity caused every blade of grass and every tree to accumulate feathery ice. It was very odd and mystical looking. I took a few pictures, but it was cold, so I didn't stay there very long.

Cold is relative. I think it only dipped below freezing, but since I only have "just enough" clothing with me to keep my pack light, I'm sometimes a bit shy of what I need. A local guy told me tonight will be the last frost, I guess we'll see.

Right now, I'm hiking with about eight others. We all do the same mileage, more or less, and end up seeing each other at shelters here and there, although none of them are at Miss Janet's right now.

Miss Janet was extremely generous. She cooked a huge breakfast for everyone who spent the night and any additional hikers who wandered by. The breakfast table was packed and followed the chaotic theme of the whole place. I was actually glad to escape Miss Janet's. It's a great stop on the trail, but total sensory overload for this only child.

I got an early start and was about a half day ahead of the group I hiked with out of Hot Springs. Hiking alone, I put in some big miles. With no plan for the day, I always seemed to hike a little further and big mileage days became the norm.

The day I left Erwin, I met One Side, Phoenix and Phoenix's dog Cody. Cody is a mellow husky who was hiking the entire AT. For the next several days, One Side would declare in the morning how far he was hiking that day, typically one shelter short of where I ended up going, but toward evening he'd roll in behind me.

One Side was in his early 20s. He had broken several bones on different occasions all on the right side of his body, so he had one good luck side and one bad luck side. He told me after he completed the trail he wanted to become a smoke jumper.

Feathery ice on Big Bald

Journal Entry
April 25

THIS WEATHER STINKS

One thing I've learned on this trip is that I don't like wind. It's too loud when it blows through the trees and it prevents you from hearing all the normal sounds of the forest. Sounds like animals breaking branches as they walk through the brush or birds chirping.

Fog is second on my list of weather I don't like. I used to think fog was mysterious, but after living in it for days, the mystery is gone. It ruins views and makes everything damp.

Right now it is both windy and foggy, and a little colder than I'd like. I'm staying at the Barn with three other hikers. The Barn isn't windproof, but seems to keep the rain out — so far. The fog of course, blows in like it owns the place.

I like the Barn. It is by far the coolest shelter on the trail that I've seen. It is large and red and its official name is the Overmountain shelter. It is named after the Overmountain Men who traveled nearby on their way to defeat the British at King's Mountain, South Carolina during the Revolutionary War.

The Barn is huge, and I've set my hammock up at one end. According to the register, the views from the Barn are great. Maybe I'll find out in the morning.

I managed to escape Erwin, but I can't say the same for the other half dozen hikers I stayed there with. I have not seen any of them since I left.

Today's hiking excitement was a climb over Roan Mountain. Roan Mountain is a 2,000-foot high bump in the ridge. It is supposed to be home to the highest shelter on the AT. I don't know if it's really true, but that's what was written in the register.

The Barn turned out to be one of the most scenic places I stayed on the AT. The next morning, the fog slowly marched out of the valley and revealed beautiful views of several nearby ridges. Soon after, huge clouds rolled in and somersaulted between the mountains.

My major conflict remained how fast I was hiking. By no means was I the fastest hiker out there, but I always wanted to make progress. Many times I would see other hikers at a shelter one night, they'd leave in the morning and I'd never see them again. Sometimes after a few days I would see their names again in a shelter register, already more than a day ahead of me.

It seemed to rain all the time or at least be overcast. At the time I figured that it was a normal spring in the East, and that I was just sensitive to the bad weather since I was outside all the time. I had no idea that I was hiking through record breaking rainfall for the season.

Journal Entry
April 26

LONGHORNS

My name is Iron Toothpick, and I'm addicted to hiking. Every day is a 20+ mile day now. A few days ago, I hiked past the 300 mile mark and today I'm over 400. I keep thinking I need to slow down, but I feel good, so I keep on going.

Not long after I left the Barn today, the fog and wind returned. Whatever.

Later, while hiking over the Roan Highlands, it cleared up a little. The Roan Highlands is a huge field of rolling hills. It's about 5,000 feet in elevation and is covered in thick grass. On a clear day, you could probably see for miles.

Cattle graze on the highlands. I wouldn't normally give them a second thought, but these cattle were actually longhorns, and like the name suggests, they were sporting huge horns like the ones some Texan would use as a hood ornament. There were also calves. This didn't look good. All the nature lore I've heard suggests that animals are most aggressive when their young are around. I tried to walk around them, but instead found myself surrounded. The hills and fog initially concealed them as I walked into their field, but as wisps of fog blew by and lifted a bit, it revealed dozens of cattle, and I was standing right in the middle of the herd.

After a few nervous minutes, and a lot of longhorn snorting, the herd finally parted around me, and I was able to escape impalement and walk out without incident.

My hammock in the loft of the Overmountain shelter ("the Barn")

I was actually fairly comfortable hiking in rain or drizzle or whatever Mother Nature had to offer. During the day, I mostly wore shorts and a t-shirt. After setting up my hammock, I would change into a dry fleece and flannel pajama bottoms. My flannel PJ bottoms were one of my luxury items, since they weighed much more than their synthetic counterparts would have.

My system worked well everyday. I could be in the rain for days and my sleeping bag and nighttime clothes stayed dry. The only unpleasant part was getting dressed in the morning. It's hard to change out of dry comfortable clothes into cold wet ones.

So, logistically, the weather had little impact on me. I packed the same way every morning, rain or shine. Of course, the rain made everything less pleasant. On sunny days I slowed a bit while hiking and lingered at scenic views. In the morning, I took longer to get going, talked with other hikers and took my time to cook breakfast. In hindsight, the poor weather actually sped up my progress along the trail. Then once the miles started adding up, I just wanted to keep adding to the pile. It was like I was collecting miles and they were in short supply.

Later in the day, I encountered my first trail relocation. Sometimes the clubs that maintain the trail elect to move it in order to give the ground a rest. When they move the trail, they post a map and tell about the new section of trail. During the relocation, five miles were replaced by seven and a half. This wasn't a big deal in the big picture, but it was the first time it dawned on me that the length of the trail can actually vary slightly from year to year.

I became concerned as I hiked through the new section, because things I saw didn't agree with the *Data Book*. I wasn't really lost, the white blazes told me I was on the AT, but I also didn't know where I was along the trail. It was disorienting. Normally, I could pinpoint my location based on the descriptions in the *Data Book*.

Even when I rejoined the old trail, I could not match up the landmarks in the book with what I saw. It started to get dark so I began looking for a place to camp. While I was scoping out the tree situation, One Side caught up.

One Side and I hiked on, probably not more than a mile, to a shelter. The shelter was in the *Data Book*, I just didn't think I had hiked that far. It ended up being a 27-mile day (some other hikers commented that it was cool that One Side and I had done a marathon that day).

At Miss Janet's I emailed Pete and Michaela a shopping list and told them when I thought I would reach the Kincora Hostel in Hampton, Tennessee. With my increased mileage, I was way ahead of schedule. My new mileage obsessed plan was to stop by Kincora, get my mail-drop and cruise on, but when I got there, I found I arrived before my mail-drop did.

It was clear I needed a new plan. I couldn't waste a day waiting for the mail, but I didn't want to miss my package either. There was a camp store about two miles away, so I stocked up on supplies there, mailed home some cold-weather gear I didn't think I would need anymore and left instructions at Kincora Hostel to forward my mail-drop up the trail a couple of hundred miles.

I met up with some other hikers who were planning a birthday party for E-Dogg. I met E-Dogg the night before while camping, but didn't realize it was her birthday. They asked me to join the celebration, which was at a local campground, and it sounded great. I could hang out with them for a little while, eat some food and then hike a few more miles in the afternoon.

It was one of the few clear days I had since leaving Georgia, and it was great to relax in the sunshine while pigging out on burgers. Somehow Tortoise, while on the trail, managed to arrange for a birthday cake to be delivered to the party. After some cake, ice cream, more burgers and a few games of basketball, I began to think I was too focused on making miles and might be missing some fun along the way.

I walked back to Kincora Hostel with E-Dogg and Montana, who were both planning on spending the night there. Montana had dominated the basketball court at the campground during lunch. He easily sank almost every shot he took and maneuvered around everyone else with ease. Part of his secret might have been that he was playing barefoot.

Montana was an interesting guy. He was one of the youngest hikers I met on the AT, around age 20. He made his own leather pack and his own moccasins, which he hiked in part of the time. The rest of the time he hiked barefoot. He started hiking the AT to pass some time, and ended up hanging out with the thru-hiker crowd. His plan was to leave the trail in Damascus, Virginia and go out to the Grand Canyon to meet his family for a rafting trip.

Montana was an expert hitchhiker. He had hitchhiked across the United States and through parts of Mexico. He casually mentioned that he was going to hitchhike from Damascus all the way to Arizona.

For me, hiking the AT was a vacation that I took to feel totally free and in control of my destiny. That was really just an illusion though. While the freedom I tasted on the trail was good, it was only temporary. In a few months it would be over, and I would return to my normal life. Montana was truly a free man doing his own thing in his own time.

My afternoon with E-Dogg and Montana made me realize how selfish I was. My selfishness manifested itself as an obsession with hiking high-mileage days. In Erwin, I had sent Pete and Michaela my shopping list with barely any lead time. Then I arrived at Kincora Hostel even earlier than I estimated and was about to leave without waiting for the mail-drop they had gone through the trouble to send. My obsessive personality had found a target to focus on.

I decided to stay at Kincora Hostel and wait for my mail-drop. Staying ended up being a good decision. I got to quiz Montana some more about his life, and I also got to meet Bob Peoples. Bob runs Kincora Hostel and knows all the trail gossip. He was fun to talk to and I enjoyed getting to know him. Later that evening, the group I hiked with out of Hot Springs arrived, including Mr. Ed and Hoser. In the morning my mail-drop arrived, complete with cookies and news from home. All was well.

Mr. Ed

"My Last Job Sucked So Bad I'm Hiking The AT" HOSER

I HIKED OUT OF KINCORA HOSTEL with Mr. Ed and Hoser. We talked about what job we left before starting the AT. Hoser worked as an industrial engineer and had helped design factories for Intel®. His contribution to the design of the buildings was to ensure that the silicon wafers flowed efficiently within the constraints of a factory setting. He told Mr. Ed and me about life at Intel. It sounded like most jobs, sometimes interesting and sometimes boring.

Intel downsized, but instead of laying off people, they offered stock to employees who wished to "retire" early. At age 27, Hoser took the stock and retired. He didn't have enough money to retire for the rest of his life, but from time to time he'd check Intel's stock price to see how long he could stay on vacation.

After completing the AT, Mr. Ed planned to take a high school teaching job in Ohio. He was worried about what kind of teacher he would be and if he'd be able to keep his students under control. Other teachers at his school assured him he wouldn't have any problems, but like any conscientious person, he was still concerned about it.

There are many reasons people hike the AT. Some are seeking higher meaning or are looking to find peace within them. My plan to hike the AT was spawned more from boredom and an unsatisfying job than the urge to seek nirvana.

For the most part, I find my career as a software programmer rewarding. I even program for fun when I'm not at work. At times, I even combine my computer geekiness with my outdoor interests.

When I started bicycling several years ago, I wondered if my training actually made me go faster. The easy and normal way to find out the answer was to time myself over a course and compare my times from week to week. I thought I could do better, so I programmed a gadget that recorded my performance and allowed me to race against past performances. The gadget would give me feedback every couple of seconds, instead of a single update when I finished the bike course.

Another thing I did was to create a web site for my friends and family, where they could track my progress on the AT. I then programmed software to receive my emailed journal entries and update my web site with them. The site even included a map showing where I was on the trail when I wrote each entry.

Before leaving for the trail, my job evolved to a point where I did less and less actual programming work and tended to do more and more bureaucratic chores. This resulted in general boredom for me eight hours a day. Boredom led to daydreaming, which in my case led to taking off a summer to hike.

After hiking most of the day, the three of us decided to camp at the Vandeventer shelter. Bob Peoples warned us that morning that the water supply at that shelter was located a half mile away and down a steep hill. We decided to stay there anyway, even though we couldn't figure out why anyone would erect a shelter so far from a water source. Upon arrival, this mystery was immediately revealed. The shelter was placed near a rocky outcrop overlooking an expansive valley. In the valley you could see some farms, a few small towns and a huge lake that extended as far as we could see. It had the best view of any shelter I had seen.

Hoser and Mr. Ed filled my water bottles in exchange for a couple of cookies from my mail-drop (they were that good).

The three of us hiked a few more days together and soon entered Virginia. It felt very satisfying to be in my home state, even though it would be another month before I hiked through Northern Virginia where I lived. Like in Hot Springs, the AT runs right through the town of Damascus and we decided to stop there for a break. It was the end of April, and 10 days since my last zero day, so I figured it was time for another. We stayed at a hostel in town, which turned out to be a good place to relax. It had a covered porch with a grill and was right on Main Street. While sitting in the shade of the porch, Hoser, Mr. Ed and I heckled other hikers as they trickled into town.

A few people had some grilling experience and we ended up having a barbeque. After eating big, the owner of a local restaurant stopped by the hostel and dropped off a couple of pans of barbequed chicken. Even more food! Things were good.

The next day, which was our zero day, was the hottest on the trail to that point. So while our laundry was washing, Hoser and I walked around in our rain gear, baking in the heat. I decided to buy a new pair of shoes. My trail runners were trouble free for the first quarter of the trail. I didn't have any blisters, any hotspots or ankle pain — they were pure shoe heaven. I'm not sure why I felt the need to get new shoes, since the old ones were working so well, but somehow I had the idea in my head that I should change my shoes every 500 miles.

The outfitter in Damascus sold the same brand of shoes I had, but not the same model. This wouldn't do. After rummaging through all the shoes, I finally spied a single box of my model. Surprisingly, the shoes were my size, but another model year than the ones I had and they looked a little different. They were as close as I could get, so I bought them.

Mr. Ed's girlfriend arrived in the afternoon. He was planning to take a few days off to go see the Kentucky Derby with her. The two of them hung out with Hoser and me for part of the day. We drove to the next town to eat Italian food, which was a bit silly since there was an Italian restaurant in Damascus. If you have access to a car, you have to use it. On the way back from dinner we stopped by a Wendy's to pick up a second dinner.

The next day, Hoser, Wild Flamingo (who had arrived in town the day Hoser and I zeroed) and I left town with a gaggle of other hikers I had seen off and on since the Smokies. I felt sluggish and my new shoes made my feet ache. I always felt tired after taking a zero day. Of course, after taking a zero day I always headed back to the trail with a ton of food in my pack. Plus, it's always an uphill walk back to the trail since towns are normally built on rivers and rivers are in valleys. Also, the break in my hiking rhythm didn't help.

Hoser and I decided that at this point, zero days were bad for us. Outside of special trail excursions, Damascus would be my last zero day.

The group we hiked with included Homebound and Psycho Heiko (who I first ran into at Cheoah Bald, just outside NOC), Short Pants (Psycho Heiko's friend who jumped onto the trail in Damascus) and Happy (who I met before Hot Springs). Pez caught up with us about mid-day. He announced that he began following a tradition set by Mountain Goat and was now cooking all his meals over an open fire.

One of the things that made Mountain Goat unique among thru-hikers was that he cooked his meals over a fire. Most hikers carried stoves, which ran on fuel of some sort (usually alcohol). Reliably making a fire, especially with the wet weather we had, took serious fire building skills. Pez and Mountain Goat hiked together for a while and Pez started learning the ways of the Mountain Goat. Pez sent his stove home since they were always cooking over a fire together.

Sadly, in Damascus, Mountain Goat had to leave the trail for a family emergency. This left Pez on his own and he wanted to keep the tradition going. The problem was that he didn't have the Mountain Goat's fire building skills.

PONIES

Today we hiked over Mt. Rogers. We saw people riding horseback and a lot of day hikers. There are wild ponies near Mt. Rogers. The ponies like to lick the sweat off of smelly hikers. They also like eating sweaty things, like the straps on your pack and the straps on your hiking poles.

I timed my hike through the highlands (which followed the ridge) to coincide with an afternoon thunderstorm. This was a little more excitement than I wanted. Lightening struck several times nearby and was all the more visible since there were few trees. Hoser went for cover, which in retrospect was the right move. I kept hiking and thinking that the descent off the highlands would begin at any moment. But the ridge kept going and going.

Luckily, I survived to hike on to Old Orchard shelter. There are a lot of good hammock spaces here. The shelters in Virginia are very nice, which is a big change from some of the ones in Tennessee, which were junky in comparison.

The rumor is that a restaurant delivers pizza to the shelter we plan to stay at tomorrow.

Hoser trying to make sense of the ponies at Mt. Rogers.

My hammock doubling as a clothesline

The pizza rumor was true. Actually, the shelter we stayed in the following night was more of a self-run hostel. It had running water, hot showers, a telephone and a soda machine. Things in Virginia kept getting better and better.

The next day I stayed in a motel in Atkins, with Hoser, Wild Flamingo and a few others. The news said that tornadoes were headed our way, but it didn't even rain. The forecast was for rain all week, but we've escaped most of it.

A few days prior, Short Pants (hiking with Psycho Heiko) found a tick. She removed it, but two days later she found a nice red spot around the location where she was bitten. In Atkins, she went to a clinic. She had a slight fever and is now being treated for Lyme disease. So we all immediately started worrying about ticks.

A diner in Atkins had an all-you-can-eat spaghetti lunch. Wild Flamingo showed his eating prowess by eating more plates than anyone at the table. Afterwards, we all lay in the grass in front of the billboard for the diner and napped. I felt pretty bad. I was as full as I have ever been in my life — so much so that I had difficulty taking a full breath. Although we all ordered the special, the service was slow. Something about the slow timing of the portions allowed us to overstuff ourselves. Homebound, who had tried to keep up with Wild Flamingo, was the worst off and ended up refunding part of his lunch. It must have been quite a sight to see a half dozen skinny hikers, looking a little sick, rubbing their bellies in front of the all-you-can-eat sign.

BLAND

Right now I'm staying outside of Bland, Virginia. Very exciting, I know.

There hasn't been anything great to report lately. I've just been hiking a lot as expected. There's been the usual deer or millipede sighting, but that's about it. Spring is finally here and the warm weather makes it nice around camp. Sending my cold-weather gear home was the right decision.

Oh, I do have good news. My new shoes finally made friends with my feet. It may not sound like a big deal, but trust me, it is.

My next big worry is Trail Days. Trail Days is a gathering of thru-hikers that will take place back in Damascus on May 17 and 18. The rumor is that it's super-easy to hitch a ride there, but that sounds a bit sketchy to me. So now I'm concerned about how I will get there.

These are the big issues I think about while hiking.

At times, hiking 2,000 miles just doesn't seem challenging enough. On the AT there are several traditional challenges. There is the four-state challenge, which is to hike in four states in a single day. There is also the half-gallon challenge, which is to eat a half-gallon of ice cream at the halfway point of the trail. Wild Flamingo came up with a new one. It was called the Pizza Hut challenge.

PEARISBURG, UGH

My dislike for the Pearisburg area started on the hike in. Wild Flamingo suggested the Pizza Hut Challenge, which was to hike the 16 miles to Pearisburg before the all-you-can-eat buffet closed.

The terrain in Virginia until that point was easy to hike. Around Pearisburg things changed. It turned rocky and had steep muddy downhill sections. For the first time, I wished I had worn hiking boots. My feet hurt more than any other time on the trip, including the "warm up" period during the first days in April. The rain last night didn't help much either and ensured that everything was slick.

Oh, I forgot to mention one detail about the challenge. We didn't know when the lunch buffet ended so we didn't have any idea if it was even possible to get there in time or if we had all day.

After eight miles of fast hiking, I told Wild Flamingo that I was out of the challenge. I felt bad for bailing on him, but I'm trying to get to Maine not Pizza Hut.

Rushing the first eight miles made the last eight seem like they took forever, but I finally made it. When I hiked into Pearisburg I found Wild Flamingo on a payphone doing something with his stocks. He had slipped on one of the muddy downhill sections and had mud stains all over one side of him. He finished up his conversation and while he thumbed for a ride, I used the phone to synch my PocketMail. Before PocketMail could finish, he found us a ride to Pizza Hut, which was three miles away.

We made the challenge (which I wasn't really a part of anymore), but I don't think it was worth it. Rushing the first part of the hike put me in a bad mood that lasted the rest of the day.

The more I learned about Pearisburg, the less I liked it as a trail stop. It's a nice place, just not easy to get around unless you have a car. "The" place to stay in town was supposed to be the hostel. It was located in the back of a residential area. The nearest phone was a half mile away, the nearest store was a half mile away and the nearest laundry facility was a mile away. Why is Pearisburg such a great trail stop?

The next day, instead of taking a zero day, we hiked six miles. Like every re-supply, the hike back to the trail was uphill, with packs full of food. This time it was also sunny and hot. I'd learned that it is time on your feet that matters and six miles was an easy day regardless of the conditions. At the shelter, we got to spend some time with the Canadians.

The Canadians were three Canadians who were runners. They were older than me (I won't guess) and they were fast. They planned to attend Trail Days and then take a break to run a race near Boston. I forgot the name of the race, but it was a multi-leg competition and some of the legs were 17 miles. When we met them they were tapering for the race which might be why we caught up to them.

The following day, the hiking got easier. There were fewer rocks and I think my feet were getting used to the battering. The trail was also more interesting.

Sometimes the AT winds endlessly through thick woods. Occasionally you'll see an animal or an unusual tree, but otherwise it is a lot of hiking in nice surroundings, but not that much different than hiking around back home. Outside Pearisburg there were streams, rolling fields, and a 300-year-old oak tree. The trail also followed a nice ridge. I wouldn't call it a knife-edge, but it was sharp by AT standards. I also met two grandmothers who were hiking the trail together.

For the most part, Hoser, Wild Flamingo and I kept together and consistently hiked big days. They actually hiked faster than me, but Wild Flamingo liked sleeping in shelters so he would stop early to secure his real estate. I was always the last of our trio to roll into camp, but we always had plenty of daylight left to lounge around camp together.

Journal Entry
May 14

FOUR PINES HOSTEL

Last night we stayed at Four Pines Hostel. It's actually a man's detached three-car garage. The man used to work at a nearby grocery store and one night a few years ago, a hiker asked him if he could set up a tent in his yard. Instead, he offered the hiker his garage for the night. Word of mouth brought more hikers and last year 950 people stayed in his "hostel." The man does not hike himself, but he seems to really enjoy hosting 10-30 hikers a night during the season. His son hung out with us after school, though we might not be the best influence on him.

I picked up another mail-drop and took a hot shower. I am now restocked with cookies (and food). I also got a note and a picture from home. The picture was from a group of my friends who all went to the beach last weekend. Since I normally would have been with them, they took a picture of themselves surrounding a life-sized wooden doll with a nametag that said "Iron Toothpick" on it.

The highlight yesterday was climbing Dragon's Tooth, which is a rocky and slightly exposed part of a mountain. In a few sections there are metal rungs bolted into the rock to help people climb up and down. It was pretty heavy duty scrambling by AT standards, a nice change of pace.

The section of the AT near Catawba, Virginia is very scenic with high vistas and wide green valleys. The rain took a hiatus for a while, and we enjoyed a string of lazy spring days with great views.

I hoped to take a few days off the trail in June to watch some friends race in a half iron distance triathlon in Cambridge, Maryland. I live near the mid-point of the AT and thought it would be a good time to take a break and visit with friends and family. When I started hiking, I had no idea if my pace would put me near home around the time of the race, but it ended up looking like it would work out perfectly.

Since I only live 40 miles from the trail, I figured if I was ahead of schedule I could walk home instead of getting a ride. There was something about walking home from Georgia that sounded cool.

McAfee Knob ▲
Catawba Valley ▶

Planning? I'm On Vacation!

BEFORE LEAVING FOUR PINES HOSTEL, I confirmed rental car plans for Trail Days and everything was a go. I was slightly skeptical about the car though, but figured I would feel better when I actually saw it waiting for me. If the car didn't show up as planned, we'd be in a bit of a bind. Hoser, Wild Flamingo and I had just enough food to get us to the car pick-up point.

Wild Flamingo turned out to be a serious planner. He was already working on a post-Trail Days plan. Based on his calculations, he told me I should pass through Northern Virginia in early June, just as I hoped. Although it was really total luck since I didn't follow any plan on the AT. In fact, having to rent a car forced me to figure out where I was going to be a week ahead of time. Easy to do, but it meant that I couldn't just take a short day because I felt bad or there was a fun place to stop.

Wild Flamingo tried to talk me out of my plan to walk home from the trail. Walking home would take two days, which would put me more than 40 miles further behind he and Hoser and it would take me longer to catch up. I wasn't sure what to think. Not walking home meant that I would need a ride home, probably from lower Pennsylvania, and then a ride back again. I was inclined to walk home.

SLEEPING DEER

After leaving the hostel, Hoser, Wild Flamingo and I took the whole day to a hike a leisurely 16 miles over easy terrain. Back in Pearisburg, I met Beaker, Mighty Mouse and Grinder and they caught up with us during the day. At one point, there was a long train of us hiking together on the trail. After a late start and taking a lot of breaks, we ended up at McAfee Knob around lunchtime. We then rested for hours there enjoying the nice day.

There was a guy at McAfee Knob making a documentary about the AT. His name was Dakota Driver. He filmed Hoser and me walking out on the cliffs with our packs. After our lame acting, we went back to relaxing and he filmed other hikers as they arrived. He said the film would be available in a year or so.

We finally hiked on and arrived at camp around 6:00 p.m. There are no flat spots near the shelter, so Hoser camped near a creek, down a hill from the shelter. It's only mildly spooky, but Hoser said he didn't want to die alone, so I'm down here now too. I'm pretty close to the creek. One tree the hammock is attached to has many of its roots in the water.

As it got dark, a herd of deer decided that they would bed down right next to us. Hoser, who hunts deer, predicted a lot of snorting and stomping around, but so far they are quiet. Much quieter than in the shelter.

Hoser and I thought it would be pretty cool if Dakota Driver was at Katahdin to tape our final summit, but that never worked out. I didn't see or even hear about him the rest of the hike. One day however, after I returned home, I was shopping at Hudson Trail Outfitters and happened to glance up at a video playing in the store. Sure enough, there was Hoser and me walking out on the cliffs at McAfee Knob.

Journal Entry
May 15

ONE THIRD

According to Wild Flamingo, we are at the one third point of the trail. To celebrate, we hiked in a thunderstorm.

We pulled into a shelter to ride it out, and I decided to stay for at least 30 minutes to ensure the last of the lightening had passed. Wild Flamingo decided to leave after five minutes. As he walked out, a bolt of lightening lit up the surrounding woods, but he just kept walking. Hoser and I ended up waiting another 45 minutes for the storm to pass.

We stopped in a town earlier today and Hoser secretly bought some beer. He then lugged them 10 miles to the next shelter and surprised us with them. So, in the pouring rain, with soaked shoes and gear, we drank cold beer and ate cookies.

My pre-dinner was actually a large candy bar and another beer, which gave me over 700 calories. Pasta and cookies followed.

Tomorrow we will cross Virginia's halfway point and hopefully meet the rental car company.

Wild Flamingo, ready for rain.

Trail Days

TRAIL DAYS

When I woke up today, my biggest concern was getting the rental car. Our plan was to walk 10 miles to a point where the AT crosses the Blue Ridge Parkway and meet the rental car company there. The hiking was easy, and we arrived an hour early. I envisioned that our meeting place was an overlook on the parkway with concessions and a parking lot. The reality was that it was just a mile marker on the road near a stone bridge.

We set our stuff out to dry on the bridge and waited. About 20 minutes before the appointed time, the driver pulled up in a mini-van. By 11:00 a.m., we were on our way to the rental office. Sweet. Not much could go wrong now. Well, there was a glitch at the rental office, but the result was that at 11:45 a.m., we drove a 15-passenger van out of Lexington, Virginia. I was very happy.

Our luck got even better. On the ramp to I-81, we saw a guy and a girl, both with backpacks, hitchhiking. They had a sign they had made, but we didn't need to read it. We pulled up, and I rolled the window down.

The two clearly had a plan. The girl was attractive and their plan was to let her do the talking. She gave us a rehearsed sales pitch on how they were hiking the AT and wanted to go to Damascus. While she was talking, I could see the gears in her head turn. Three unshaven guys…the driver wearing a Patagonia® long underwear top for a shirt….hey, these guys might be going to Trail Days too! We interrupted her speech and they piled in. They were happy to have any easy hitch all the way to Damascus, and we were happy to fill the spacious van with more stinky hikers.

The hitchhikers' names were 2-Step and Notes. Notes was a reporter for a Chattanooga newspaper. The paper was running a series about his trip, and his girlfriend met him in Damascus with a bunch of recent articles. His series was front page news and included photos and graphics showing where he was on the trail.

On the way down I-81, we stopped at a truck stop to do laundry and shower. We arrived in Damascus late in the afternoon and hung around town together and ate dinner. It was difficult to walk around town because everywhere we went we saw people we hiked with and stopped to catch up. It's sort of hard to describe the odd bond I felt with many of the other hikers. I felt like I knew them really well, yet I only knew most of them for a few days.

By the time we got to the campsite, it was dark and the party, such as it was, was going. Damascus wisely puts the official campsite for Trail Days about a mile outside of town. There was a lot of drinking around a lot of campfires. There were also people playing the bongos here and there, but overall the whole scene was pretty lame. A few people would try to get things going for a while, but it never seemed to work, so it ended up being mostly a bunch of drunk people staring into campfires.

Tent City at Trail Days

Overall, I found Trail Days to be a bust. I think Hoser, Wild Flamingo and I all knew that it would be before we went. For some reason though, we felt we had to witness it.

Trail Days wasn't all bad though. It gave us a chance to see other hikers we hadn't seen or heard of in weeks or over a month and find out where they were and how their hikes were going. I found the rafters who, up until a week or so before Trail Days, were still hiking together. Windtalker was even sporting freshly started dreadlocks.

Journal Entry
May 18

TRAIL DAYS — RELOADED

The second day of Trail Days (Sunday) was much more fun than the day before. I saw Happy and Happy had a Mr. Ed sighting. Mr. Ed wasn't at Trail Days, but Happy said he was hiking Mach speed to catch up to us. The question is — will he pass us while we're at Trail Days?

During the day there was an expo of sorts. At the campground they had vendors that would fix equipment (e.g. LEKI would fix and tune up your hiking poles, Mountain Safety Research would checkout and clean your stove, etc.) and in the park they had some outfitters, and more vendors like Hennessy Hammock and GoLite showing their new stuff and answering questions.

In the afternoon there was a hiker parade, which was a bit odd. The one float was a Pepsi® delivery truck. All of the hikers walked in the parade, then the last half was every emergency vehicle in Damascus.

After all the festivities, we decided to crash with the non-Canadians (Beaker, Grinder and Mighty Mouse), who were staying in the same motel with the Canadians.

We stayed in a motel that night and watched the last few rounds of the National Spelling Bee on ESPN and then went to see a movie.

The non-Canadians drove down to Trail Days with the Canadians. The six of them crammed into a normal size rental car with their packs. It sounded like a long, cramped ride. The Canadians were leaving at 6:00 a.m. to return to where they left the trail. The non-Canadians, Wild Flamingo, Hoser and I got back to the motel after the movie at about midnight. With the huge van at our disposal, the decision was obvious and the non-Canadians rode back to the trail with us.

After breakfast, we picked up 2-Step and left Damascus. On the way back to the trail we stopped at a restaurant called the Home Place. The Home Place is one of those "AT Classics" that everyone talks about. It is only open a few days a week and was closed when we passed through Catawba the first time.

Lunch at the Home Place was excellent. They only offer family style all-you-can-eat. Ordering is simple; everyone at the table decides what meats they want. That's it. The staff then proceeds to bring out dish after dish of the kind of food you'd expect from a place called the Home Place (mashed potatoes, green beans, etc.). We tried to represent thru-hikers well and ate as much as we could.

The next stop was a Kroger grocery store so that everyone could re-supply. The debate, as usual, was how much food to take. Usually I knew before I went into a store exactly what I wanted. This time I winged it. I ended up flipping through the *Data Book* and shopping at the same time.

The non-Canadians were planning to hike after our Kroger visit, but it was raining and getting late, so Beaker lobbied for a hotel room in Daleville. 2-Step elected to stay with us, so seven of us ended up sharing a room.

While Hoser and I scoped out the room, the long lost Mr. Ed came barging in. He just happened to be staying in the room next to us. So, we didn't have to chase Mr. Ed to Maine. The spot where we left the trail was only about 20 miles north of Daleville, so we figured he'd catch up to us just before I left the trail in June.

Trail Days was the longest break I'd taken and it was nice to return to the trail routine. Increasingly, I found that I'd rather be on the trail than in town, although I was looking forward to my mid-trail vacation at home for a week.

Hoser and Wild Flamingo encounter a southbounder

IT'S GOOD TO BE BACK

After a couple of days off, I couldn't wait to get back on the trail. The forecast was for a week of rainy days, but I didn't care. The AT seems like the right place for me to be right now.

We dropped off 2-Step and the car and were back on the trail at 10:00 a.m. It would have been a little earlier, but some of the roads were flooded. Luckily, the driver from the car rental place knew the back roads well.

It feels good to be back to the simple life and the time away did wonders for my energy level. I cruised even with a heavy pack.

Lately, I've lost my fixation with pack weight. This has opened me up to three things:

First, Waldies®. The fad on the AT this year is Waldies, and after 700 miles, I've finally joined in. Waldies are 3.5 oz. rubber clogs with air holes all over the top that people wear around camp. Now I have tried them, and I'm more than happy to carry the weight. While in camp, my feet can relax and dry while my shoes air out.

Second, more water. I've ditched my adventure race-ish water bottle scheme (two Gatorade bottles strapped to the front of my shoulder straps). I now use a plastic bladder and have twice the capacity. It means more weight, but it also means I don't have to stop and sample every water source on the AT.

Third, I've decided to go stove-less and only eat cold food. It's an experiment I'm doing over the next few weeks. We'll see how it goes. I sent my stove and cooking pot home and bought several pounds of bagels.

The plus for "no-cook" is that it is much easier. I eat the moment I get into camp. There's no fiddling with a stove, getting water, etc. I just open a bag of bagels and open a squeeze bottle of peanut butter and dinner is served.

One con to "no-cook" is that the food is heavy. This is slightly offset by not carrying fuel, a stove and my cooking pot. As long as I can re-supply often, the weight penalty for "no-cook" is low. Of course, my experiment opened up with supplies for six days, so I'm carrying my heaviest pack to date.

So far I like the "no-cook" scheme. The last two days were perfect for hiking and camping, despite the grizzly forecast. A "Welcome Back" from the trail.

Today Hoser and I saw a turkey and its chicks. I caught a glimpse of one earlier in the day as it flew off, but this one just walked away quickly while its babies hurried as best they could up a hill away from us. That was our wildlife excitement (of course, right now deer are snorting at something outside so things might get more interesting).

The next day was my worst day yet on the AT. I had low moments since starting my hike, but that day was the lowest.

Several factors were involved. First, it rained all day. It had rained before and it usually didn't bother me, but I'm sure it contributed to my bad mood. Second, my feet were wet all day. One drawback to wearing trail running shoes is that when it rains, your feet get wet. Third, it was my second 25 mile day in a row. By itself, 25 miles or two 25-mile days wasn't a big deal, but I found out that 25 miles in wet shoes makes for a painful day. I guess wet feet don't tolerate as much abuse as dry ones.

Although I was in extreme pain for most of the day, I felt I had to keep going because we planned to hike to a specific shelter. This, I didn't like.

Hoser and I let Wild Flamingo do the planning. This started when we planned to rent the car to go to Trail Days. While I don't like to plan, it was necessary then since we needed to let the car rental office know where to pick us up.

The problem with planning a week out on the AT is that you don't know what the weather and trail surface will be like. So I found myself committed to 25 miles even though it was raining and the trail surface was mainly wet rocks, which slows me down. I would have rather taken a long break during the day and ended up shortening the day.

So there I was, totally miserable, wanting to take a break, with no way to tell Wild Flamingo or Hoser that I wouldn't be at the shelter. That made me more miserable. I also started thinking about my mid-trail break. I realized I had my dates wrong and that instead of going home the following week, it would be the week after. I was excited to see everyone at home and realizing that it would be twice as long before I went home didn't help my mood.

TOO MANY MILES

We are moving fast, and at this pace I figure that we will probably be in Boiling Springs, Pennsylvania on the day I want to go home. I wrote an email (that has since been retracted), asking who would like to drive to Pennsylvania during a workday to pick up three stinky hikers. Today, I realized that I was getting too caught up in the trail and too caught up in making miles.

My new plan is to slow down a bit. I'm going to stay in Waynesboro, Virginia and be in Shenandoah National Park the last part of Memorial Day weekend. I'll also be able to stop at Sky Meadows State Park, where I visited the AT just before leaving in April. I'll probably camp there, which I would not normally do in "trail mode" since the campground is 1.3 miles from the trail.

This slowdown means that I'll stop hiking with Hoser and Wild Flamingo. While I'm home, I plan to pick them up (from Pennsylvania somewhere) and take them to Washington, D.C. I don't know if I'll see them after that.

I'm a little sad. I first met Hoser at the North Carolina border, 725 miles ago. I met Wild Flamingo the day before I hiked into NOC.

We'll see, there's still a lot of trail to go.

Solo

*I*T WAS VERY SAD TO BREAK AWAY from Hoser and Wild Flamingo. They were good to hang out with in camp, and we all had the same attitude about how long to stay in towns and what shelters and campsites to stay at.

We had a pretty regular routine on the trail. Wild Flamingo liked to sleep in shelters and would usually arrive early enough to score a shelter spot. Hoser and I were a bit anti-shelter and would roll in and set up camp near the shelter. In the mornings, Wild Flamingo liked to get a very early start. I think he woke up just before dawn, which in the summer is pretty early. He'd quietly make breakfast and pack up, trying not to disturb the other folks in the shelter. Before hiking out of camp he would swing by my hammock to wake me up.

Hoser and I would end up leaving camp around the same time, but Hoser hiked faster. When I stopped for lunch I would usually see him, just as he was finishing his lunch. It was a good system, but the miles were just a bit too long for me, so I decided to break away.

The next morning I slept in, uncertain what I would do in solo mode. There was a note in the shelter that said there was a free lunch opportunity two miles up the trail. I was in no hurry and woke up as the last person was leaving the shelter.

FREE LUNCH

There is such a thing as a free lunch. I had one today at the Dutch Haus. I'm slowing down and decided to see what the free lunch was all about. The Dutch Haus is in Montebello, Virginia. They advertise free lunches to hikers and even shuttle you off the mountain to their place.

I headed down the road to where the shuttle left. There I saw the sign for the shuttle, but it also said that the car was in the shop and that there wouldn't be any today.

I had to decide. Hike to Montebello (2.2 miles) knowing that I would have to hike back, or keep hiking the AT. I decided to see what Montebello was all about.

The free lunch was good. It was the best meal to date on the trail. Earl, the guy who runs the place, said his car would be out of the shop that afternoon and that he could pick me up 10 miles down the trail so I could stay the night. I decided to hike back to the trail, hike the 10 miles and wait for Earl.

The question was: Should I slack pack? It wasn't really a question; it was the obvious thing to do. Slack packing is hiking with just a daypack and a snack. Although it was the obvious thing to do, I left with my full pack, three days of food and all.

I don't know what was in the lunch, but it powered me up to the trail from Montebello and across the 10 miles of the AT in record time.

Now I'm back at the Dutch Haus. I'm showered and in a nice bathrobe, while THEY are doing my laundry. Pretty nice. I'm not sure why this place isn't an AT legend yet.

Tomorrow I'm going to Rusty's, a long-time AT legend. Like Trail Days or Miss Janet's, I don't think I'll be a huge fan, but I feel compelled to check it out anyway.

Oh, one more thing. I have a raging case of athlete's foot. Hikers are dirty and there are a lot of fungi around. Somehow I avoided it until recently. Now, with the constant damp conditions in my shoes, the fungi are taking over. Just thought you would like to know.

The Dutch Haus was a good place to get cheered up. After eating three good meals and doing my laundry, I felt good. I had never had the opportunity to slack pack before, but I had seen other hikers do it. Sometimes around the campfire the subject of slack packing would come up. The question was always, "Should you or shouldn't you?" I was on the non-slack packing side, although I didn't think it should be a fineable offense like some purists did.

After pondering the issue, I decided not to slack pack, mostly because I wanted to have the option of saying that I hadn't done it. I also decided that in the future I could hike without my supply of food, but that I wanted my gear to make the entire trip with me. Thus, I formed my own slack packing guidelines.

The guidelines were completely ridiculous though, since much of my gear would be mailed home or sent ahead depending on the weather outlook. On top of that, I'd really be out for a day hike, since I'd leave a nice civilized place like the Dutch Haus, hike for the day and return for the night. Not most people's idea of an epic adventure, more like a vacation.

While at the Dutch Haus, I met a group of detectives from Montgomery County, Maryland that I heard about on the trail. The rumor was that there were three, but really there were two and they hiked with a third non-detective friend. They were really nice guys, and I asked the question that probably everyone else does, "What do you do when all of those potheads light up?" They said it doesn't happen that often since the word is out about what they do for a living.

During the night, one of the detectives became violently ill, so he wasn't too talkative at breakfast. The day before I arrived at the Dutch Haus, another hiker who showed up was very sick and was taken to the hospital. There was clearly some illness going around.

RUSTY'S

Rusty's Hard Times Hollow is one of those classic places on the AT that everyone says you must see. It is three miles off the trail though, which normally would cause me to skip it. This AT classic turned out to be well worth the walk and did not disappoint.

The Rusty's experience begins about halfway down his driveway. First, there is a "Keep Out" sign. This is followed by dozens of other signs. They are not the standard signs you can buy in a store, they are custom signs that detail various rules you must follow at Rusty's. Things like, "No Guns," "No Drugs," "Dogs must be kept on a leash and can't stay more than one night," etc. The signs are all in different styles, all cleverly worded, and all professionally made.

The signs on the driveway are just a warm-up. Rusty has signs everywhere around his house, his porch, the bunkhouse, the springhouse, everywhere. There are even signs on top of signs. The signs say what you can do, and more often, what you can't do.

Rusty wasn't home when I arrived, but anyone who could read English could figure out what to do. Following the direction of the sign on the door to the front porch, I signed in and promptly put my gear in the bunkhouse.

When I signed in, I noticed that Wild Flamingo and Hoser signed in yesterday. When I mentioned Rusty's earlier in the week, they were reluctant to stop there, but said they would if I wanted to so that we wouldn't break up the team. Now that the team was broken up, I figured they would skip it.

Then, Wild Flamingo came out of the house onto the porch. Odd, since I figured he'd be long gone by now. It turns out that he felt sick this morning and he and Hoser decided to zero. Hoser was in town running errands with Rusty.

So, like a bad breakup, we're back together after one day.

Candid photos of hikers cover the walls and ceilings at Rusty's

Rusty came home a little later. With all of the rules posted, I felt like I was on thin ice. It turned out that Rusty is totally cool, not out to bust you for not following a posted rule, although he'll gently remind you.

The first thing he did after meeting me was take my picture. He had Polaroids of almost every hiker that has been through his place. The Transcontinental Bike Trail also runs near his house, so there were a few photos of bikers too. He put the Polaroids on the ceiling of the back porch. A few years ago the porch ceiling was full and he took them all down and put them into several books. Now the ceiling is filling up again. Thousands of hikers have stopped there over the years.

Rusty was really into pictures. The Polaroid portraits were just a start. The walls and ceilings were covered with candid photos of folks having fun at Rusty's. The privy was even wallpapered with pictures. It looked like there have been a lot of good times at Rusty's.

We took it easy for a couple of hours, eating pasta and peanut butter sandwiches. Rusty let us hang out in his house because there was heat and it was cold and rainy out. A few signs pointed out that first-time visitors are normally not allowed in his house.

So Rusty's turned out to be very eclectic, easily worth the walk. The place had none of the normal hiker amenities: no phone, no Internet, no electricity, and no running water, just volumes of character. Unfortunately, after returning from my hike, I heard that Rusty's Hard Times Hollow closed to hikers.

Hoser may not agree with how cool Rusty's was. He started getting flu-like symptoms that night. We stayed on the second level of the barn. Hoser woke up every half hour, ran out, ran down the slick metal stairs (slick because it was raining, as it always did), and over to the stinky privy. Not good times for Hoser.

The next morning Hoser was in bad shape. We debated what to do. It was the end of May, but cold and rainy. Staying at Rusty's didn't seem that appealing, and we didn't get the idea that Rusty would want to drive us to a hotel. Hoser decided he was well enough to hike to Waynesboro, 20 miles away. After a few miles though, he felt worse and decided to try to hitch a ride into Waynesboro.

Wild Flamingo and I continued on. The terrain was easy and we arrived in Waynesboro early in the afternoon. We met Hoser at a hotel that was just off of the AT. He was recovering, but still very sick. He planned on zeroing at the hotel to recover.

MY TURN

Wild Flamingo left early today, as is usual for him. It was pouring, and the forecast for the next week was for the same old rain and cool weather. This weather is taking the fun out of the hike. I want a refund.

I slept in and left a couple of hours after Wild Flamingo. The weather broke a bit, and the sun even came out occasionally. It was a nice change of pace.

I didn't move too fast and felt a bit odd. The whole time I was thinking of the miserable night that Hoser had at Rusty's.

After walking five miles, I crossed Skyline Drive. I didn't want to be sick in the woods, so I tried to hitch a ride back to the hotel. After an hour without any luck, I started the five-mile walk to the hotel via the road.

I started to feel really bad and sat down on the side of the road. When a car would go by I would hopelessly throw my thumb out. I don't think many locals drive on Skyline Drive, just tourists. Tourists are probably less likely to pick up hitchhikers in some place new to them. Plus, most cars were already packed with luggage and people. It wasn't looking good. Finally, some folks from Lynchburg picked me up.

At the hotel I found Hoser and got into the room, just in time. I don't think I really said much to him. I just rushed to the bathroom and puked. Somehow my body held out until the last possible moment. I won't go into the rest of the details, but I might zero here tomorrow. Ugh.

So it was my turn to get sick. At least I was in a place with indoor plumbing. It wasn't fun, and I gained more appreciation for just how bad it must have been to be sick at Rusty's. The good news was that whatever the sickness was, it passed fast. By that evening I was feeling closer to normal. The only lingering symptom was that my stomach had become more sensitive and eating anything besides soup caused a lot of intestinal pain. No big deal, how important is eating?

Hoser and I left Waynesboro the next day. Hoser hitchhiked to where he left the trail about 20 miles south, and I got a hitch so I didn't have to re-hike the five miles into Shenandoah National Park. Since I hadn't eaten much, I was low on energy and the going was slow. The trail through Shenandoah is known as one of the easiest sections, but I needed a lot of rest.

The hiking didn't help my recovery. After arriving in camp I didn't have energy to set up my hammock, I didn't have an appetite, and it was cold. I curled up in my sleeping bag on the shelter floor to rest for an hour and then managed to choke down 800 calories of food. Soon it started to get dark, and I needed to set up my hammock.

The easiest place to set it up was between a tree and the bear pole. A bear pole is a 20 foot high pole, like a flagpole. At the top it has hooks to hang your food. Hanging your food is a bit tricky. There is a smaller detachable pole that also has a hook on it. You use this smaller pole to raise your food bag to one of the hooks on the main pole. Most people don't look forward to hanging their food. Dodging a hammock strung up to the main pole wouldn't have made the process any easier.

I came to my senses and passed on hooking my hammock to the bear pole. But I was tired beyond belief and didn't feel like scouting out a new place for it. So I shoehorned it in between two tents that were already set up for the night. Luckily, the occupants didn't give me any grief for setting up my combination tripwire/clothesline/hammock in the middle of their area. Even if they did, I wouldn't have noticed.

The next morning I continued to be in complete denial of my situation and continued to hike at a crawl and not eat.

At the Loft Mountain camp store I tried to find some food that appealed to me. They were fresh out of applesauce and soups. At that point, I should have called someone from home to come get me off the trail. Having sent my stove home, I couldn't prepare anything my digestive system might agree with, like soup. Still in denial, I bought a bag of hotdog buns and headed out.

I cut the day short to give myself more time to eat, but couldn't manage to get much down. Hoser arrived, mostly recovered from his bout with the illness, and in hot pursuit of Wild Flamingo.

That night my whole body ached like I have never felt before. I didn't know what was going on, but it was time to get off the trail and recover properly.

I was about a three hour drive from home and about a week away from my scheduled hiatus. In my hammock, with my entire body in an achy pain, it was an easy decision to go home early. The next question was how to get there.

On the Appalachian Trail it is rare to be more than 30 miles from a road. I felt that if I needed to bail out, I could always gut out a long day and get to civilization. Being sick, and being reduced to a crawl put things in a different perspective. Six miles seemed like an impossible feat.

I woke up feeling a little better, but remembered the promise I made to myself during the night. I hated to go because I was 100 miles short of the point where I planned to get off the trail for my trail hiatus. But feeling ill on the trail is no fun, and I wasn't going to cover 100 miles in a week at the rate I was going.

I didn't know how I would get home since I was in the middle of the woods. Hitchhiking is always an option, especially in the Shenandoah (although it is illegal) since Skyline Drive and the AT crisscross many times. Where I was sleeping I was only two-tenths of a mile at most from Skyline Drive. I wasn't looking forward to hitching in the rain in an area where there were only tourists during the week. However, I learned that on the trail, given a few hours, everything always works out.

Among the people packed in or near the shelter where some folks from Indianapolis. Three generations of their family were section hiking the Shenandoah. The eldest, Tom, was the campground host for Big Meadows. He and his wife had been volunteering for three years in the Shenandoah. While the men (Tom, his two sons, and one of his grandsons) were section hiking, Tom's wife was holding down the campsite.

The Indianapolis Four (as I called them) were still working the kinks out of their gear and planned to call Tom's wife for a gear exchange. They said I could ride back to Big Meadows with her. We had to walk a few miles, but only a few, and the miles were on the AT (not along the road hitchhiking). I felt better knowing I had a good plan.

The Indianapolis Four provided some lucky trail magic. Just what I needed, when I needed it, where I needed it.

My parents picked me up in the afternoon, and I spent the night at their place in my old room.

HOME EARLY

So now I'm home in my own house. This morning I feel better, but eating a full meal got my stomach going again and erased any regret I had about leaving the trail.

At first I felt bad for leaving the trail early. I felt like I was going to get behind some phantom schedule. Even while on the trail the last few days, I was frustrated because progress was not what I was accustomed to. How would I ever get to Maine?

For the first time I did some serious calculations. How fast have I been going? How much longer would it take to get to Maine at that rate? When would I get there? When would I get there with a two-week break? It turns out that at the rate I have been going, it will be no problem, even with the two week break. I can relax.

Mr. Ed, Hoser and Wild Flamingo in Washington, DC

Iron Toothpick's Hostel

I INVITED HOSER AND WILD FLAMINGO to my place for a zero day. The plan constantly changed, ranging from all of us taking the train from Harpers Ferry, West Virginia to me walking home from the trail and picking them up a few days later.

When I decided to slow down I gave Hoser and Wild Flamingo my phone number. We also gave Mr. Ed an invitation via the shelter registers. When I left the trail we were all spread out. Wild Flamingo was two days ahead of me. Hoser had just caught up with me, and we had no idea where Mr. Ed was.

After being home a few days I got a call. Wild Flamingo, Mr. Ed, and Hoser were all together at Terrapin Station Hostel near Front Royal, Virginia. Wild Flamingo had developed an unusual and painful bump on his shin. He took off a day to get it looked at, so Hoser caught up to him. Meanwhile, Mr. Ed was going Mach speed and arrived at Terrapin Station on the same day Hoser did.

The doctor told Wild Flamingo to take some days off, so I drove to Front Royal, Virginia and took him to my house. A couple of days later, I picked Hoser and Mr. Ed up from Harpers Ferry.

We spent a very exciting next day in Washington, D.C. It rained of course; at that point I wouldn't have had it any other way. Wild Flamingo tested out his leg as we walked around the monuments in D.C. After posing with cavemen for some photos at the Natural History Museum, we went back home.

Wild Flamingo still had some pain, but decided to go back to the trail the next morning. Mr. Ed and I saw him off in Front Royal.

Hoser decided he wanted another zero day. We had walked all over the National Mall, and I think he wanted a true zero day. While he didn't walk, he and Mr. Ed did vacuum the entire house, took out the trash, and did the dishes. Great guests.

The next night I ate dinner with my folks and my grandparents. I brought Mr. Ed and Hoser along so my family could meet real AT hikers. I hoped that by meeting a couple of people I was hiking with, my family would feel more connected with my AT experience.

After dinner we stayed up way past our bedtime to watch New Jersey beat The Mighty Ducks.

The next morning, Mr. Ed and I dropped off Hoser in Harpers Ferry. I thought about how it might be the last time I saw him.

I then drove up to Annapolis, Maryland (a little over an hour away) to drop off Mr. Ed for a wedding he had hoped to attend. I went on to Cambridge, Maryland from there to watch some friends compete in a half iron distance triathlon. On the way to Annapolis, Mr. Ed got a taste of the D.C. area's worst traffic.

Journal Entry
June 6

FROM THE GLASGOW INN, CAMBRIDGE, MARYLAND

Today is Friday. On Monday, I plan to be back on the trail. I think Mr. Ed plans on being on the trail Sunday night. So in a couple of days we'll all be back on the trail, but in different places.

I'll be way back in the Shenandoah, Wild Flamingo will be near Harpers Ferry, possibly just as Mr. Ed gets on the trail. Hoser will be in the middle of Pennsylvania.

It will be a while before I see any of those guys again, if I do at all. When I get back on the trail it will be a new trail with new people.

When I first started the trail I was filled with anxiety, not sure if the trail was for me. Right now I'm very eager to get back.

I did some basic planning. I'm not yet at the halfway point. After all this time I can't believe I still have over half of the trail left. It's like looking in the cookie jar and seeing that it's still more than half full. Good times await.

The rain doesn't bother me day to day. It is a bit of a drag when setting up and taking down camp. Far worse is that when it rains I don't feel like hanging out. Nobody sits and stares over a vista when it's raining. When it is raining, nobody relaxes and eats lunch at a waterfall or hangs out on a high knob to take in the view.

I think the saddest part about the rainy weather is that it deprives us of that time spent just relaxing and also of the views that the trail designers went out of their way to show people.

Good or bad, it is raining a lot. That's just how it is. I trust that Mother Nature can't keep this rain up. How fast does moisture get into the air in the first place? How much moisture could possibly be left?

Wild Flamingo and Mr. Ed making themselves at home in my kitchen

I was glad I incorporated my break into my trip, but after two weeks off of the trail, I was very eager to get back. Now I see that urgency to get back to the trail differently. Some of the urge stemmed from the comfort that the trail's simple life provides. Much of the urge stemmed from the timing. My trail experience was defined as much by people as by the rocks and dirt I walked on. Those people were on the move, and if I waited too long, I'd miss the train.

Town stops are a constant reminder of how simple life on the trail is. On the trail my routine is the same everyday. The only variation might be that on dry sunny days I put a few things on the outside of my pack instead of inside. Otherwise the routine on the trail requires zero thought.

During the day, life on the trail is at its simplest. The AT is well established and marked by white blazes. There is no need for a map. No need for a compass. No need for thought.

Compared to trail life, town life is very hectic. In town I do laundry, possibly track down a store or post office with my mail-drop, buy groceries, etc. My stuff is all over the place.

In camp everything has a place. My hammock is up, my sleeping bag is in it, my food bag is in a tree, and the few odds and ends that are left are in my pack, which is clipped to the hammock.

Leaving camp I never worry about leaving stuff behind. The pack gets packed the same way it was packed the last 50 times. When leaving, I take a quick look over the ground and feel confident that I have left nothing behind. Leaving town though, I do worry. Although by the next morning the worry is over. If I was missing anything, it would have been obvious.

Being at home was the ultimate town stop. Very hectic compared to the weeks before. In the first couple of hours at my parents' place, I had showered, done my laundry and had food available. Then I went to my own house. Soon my house was full of hikers and I had planning to do for the last half of the hike. There were a lot of groceries to buy, there were mail-drops to prepare and mail out, and other mail-drops to prepare for Pete and Michaela.

Being home offered me the opportunity to better plan the contents of my mail-drops for the second half of the trail. For the first half, I didn't know how frequently I'd need supplies sent and what I would need at each point. For the second half, I knew what I wanted. I created two special mail-drops that contained sections of the *Companion* that I would need, as well as personal items such as a new toothbrush, toothpaste and batteries.

It was fun to run a hiker hostel for a few days. It was good to mix my new hiking friends with local friends and family. I also enjoyed hanging out in Cambridge and watching friends race in their triathlon. Overall, it was good to be home. In fact, it was such a good time that after reaching Maine, I planned to return home instead of hitchhiking across the country.

After talking to Montana, I made a sarcastic remark in a few emails to family and friends about hitchhiking across the U.S. When I mentioned that I was coming home after finishing the AT, a few people, including my mom, were relieved.

Wild Flamingo and Hoser at the Lincoln Memorial

Hightop Mountain

Back On The Trail

I'M BACK

It's good to be back. The trail welcomed me with warm temperatures, light breezes, and sunshine. This isn't the trail I remember.

My dad dropped me off at Powell Gap, where I left the trail two weeks ago. During my break I decided to give up the "no cook" experiment and returned to the trail with my stove.

I walked 15 miles and felt good. I bought new shoes while I was home and that, combined with not hiking for a couple of weeks, gave me some minor foot aches, but nothing unexpected.

Today I saw a bobcat. He was trotting southbound on the AT. I thought bobcats were much bigger, he was just a little bit bigger than a house cat. I also saw a turtle, and what might have been a bear, but it was gone in a flash.

I pulled into the shelter and there was only one person there. When I left the trail the shelters were overflowing with people. The sun comes out and everybody is gone.

I was a little nervous of the other guy at the shelter. There was nothing strange about him, it was just odd that he was the only one there when I expected a crowd. I found out that his name was Joey and that he was from Baltimore. I ate my Subway sub and knew I was safe. If he was the killing type, he would have done the deed before I ate the fresh sub.

Joey is hiking from Pearisburg to Harpers Ferry. He told me that a copperhead snake bit him yesterday. Just as I was thinking that this was one tough and/or crazy dude, he mentioned that the snake bit his sandal.

BEARS AND BUGS

Both the bears and bugs were out today. As I write this, I'm being eaten alive, by bugs.

Today was a busy day. I hiked almost 27 miles. I probably shouldn't have hiked so far after the time off but it's too late now.

The day started off with three deer visiting me while I packed up. They were very friendly, and I had to shoo them away from my stuff.

Soon after I started hiking, I saw my first bear. The bear initially rushed off, but then stopped and cranked his head toward me to see what I was doing. After a bit we both went on our separate ways.

I passed through Big Meadows and found Tom (whose wife gave me a ride to Big Meadows when I was sick). I thanked him for the ride and he was glad to see that I was back on the trail.

Later, I stopped by Skyland Resort and visited their dining room. They have the fastest service on the planet. My food was out instantly, no joke. I thought they might be trying to get rid of me, since I was a stinky thru-hiker, but I noticed everyone was served fast.

The meal, which was huge, slowed me down a bit in the afternoon. After some slow miles, I passed Thortons Gap and camped a mile or so north, at Pass Mountain Hut.

I found the Canadians at the shelter. Two of the three of them continued their hike, while the third decided to stay home after their race. It was good to see thru-hikers that I recognized.

The sky began to develop a rainy look which motivates me to set up my hammock. I hung it near a tent that belonged to two ladies who are starting a southbound hike of Shenandoah National Park. They happened to cook too much macaroni and cheese and offered me some. People are so nice.

Tomorrow I plan to hike to Terrapin Station. I haven't heard from Wild Flamingo, so I assume he's okay. After I pass Terrapin Station, I'll be able to read the journal entries he wrote on his first few days back. I hope his leg is better.

I didn't know it at the time, but my shoes were a big problem and they were tearing my feet up. Early on, I assumed that it was because my feet became soft during my two week break. Later, much later, I determined that the shoes just weren't right for my feet. It was a painful lesson that got worse each day. The pain developed slowly and it took me hundreds of miles to realize what is obvious now. I needed different shoes.

Deer visiting camp

ENOUGH BEARS ALREADY

Early in the day, an older man caught up to me on the trail. He walked up while I was checking out some deer, one of which was a very tiny fawn. I pointed out the deer and he went on a rant. He said he had seen enough deer, bears, fawns, bear cubs... He didn't break stride and continued listing off the animals he had enough of as he zoomed off.

As the day went on, I decided that I'd be fine if I didn't see another bear. I wasn't tired of them, just scared of what might happen if I got too close to one.

My feet also started hurting badly. Nothing serious, just intense achy pain. I guess the days off softened my feet. Descents really got the pain going.

On the last descent of the day I heard a noise in the woods. I clanked my hiking poles together like I've done dozens of times. Noises in the woods are usually from deer. I looked over my shoulder in the direction of the noise and saw two cubs scurry up two nearby trees. This could be bad.

They say that you don't want to be near a mother and her cubs, so I was concerned. They also say you should face the bear and back away. But there was a snag.

I was at the apex of a sharp switchback. The mother and cubs were inside the switch back. Both backtracking and continuing along the trail would get me closer to the bears. Hmmmm.

It was worse than that. The switch-back was there for a reason. The trail was on a steep slope, and there were many fairly large fallen trees right at the apex of the switch back. In fact, I was backed up to one of those trees. I remember thinking that at least my intense foot pain was gone.

Normally I would freeze and wait for the wildlife to go on its way. This works for longhorns, foxes, snakes, etc. The problem here was that the cubs were up in trees. Momma wasn't going anywhere.

Momma started making some huffing sounds which made me think that I should do something besides stand there. I clumsily climbed over the trees behind me, keeping a lookout behind me. After a few minutes I was deep in the woods, far from the trail but I felt safer.

I eventually hooked up with the trail again and the foot pain came back. Things were back to normal.

I hiked into Terrapin Station Hostel. It is very nice. It has a stocked fridge, and the place is very clean.

Photograph of black bear cub Tony Campbell/ Eagle Eye Imaging

My hammock in a barn in Sky Meadows State Park

"I Found What I've Been Looking For, Now I'm Going Home"

ANONYMOUS, FOUND IN A SHELTER REGISTER IN VIRGINIA

*T*HERE IS A LOT OF INFORMATION on the Internet about the AT, including a large collection of online journals. Before I left for my hike, I read many of these journals, especially from people who quit the trail.

In a few cases people leave the AT because they don't like it. These people have no regrets and the trail was just another thing in life that they sampled. You sample things in life, some things you like, others you don't like.

A few journals were filled with regret. It seemed like some mysterious illness took over toward the end. The focus would shift from talk of waking up to sunrises and birds chirping to talk of how many days in a row it had rained, or how tired they felt. I read these journals looking for clues. I wondered what started the chain of events that caused them to become negative, and to ultimately leave the trail. Could that happen to me?

At Terrapin Station, I bumped into a hiker who was in the middle of making his decision to quit the trail.

TRAIL CASUALTY

Last night there was only one other hiker at Terrapin Station Hostel. I'll call him "Greg." Yesterday morning Greg packed up, put on his shoes and headed back to the AT. Somewhere during the half-mile hike back to the trail he stopped, turned around, and walked back to the hostel.

When I arrived I found Greg on the couch. An empty pint of Ben & Jerry's ice cream was on the floor next to him. His pack and hiking poles were by the door, ready to go. Greg was considering dropping out. No injuries, no equipment problems, he had just had enough.

This morning as I was leaving, Greg was still on the couch in front of the TV where he slept. He planned to take another zero day today and think about things. Grateful Greenpeace Guy (GGG), who runs Terrapin Station, talked to Greg about his options. GGG has hiked several long trails and has a flexible attitude. GGG seems like the right guy for Greg to talk to.

I don't know what the outcome will be and probably never will. It was hard to watch. Greg is the first person I've been around while they were in the middle of making the decision to quit.

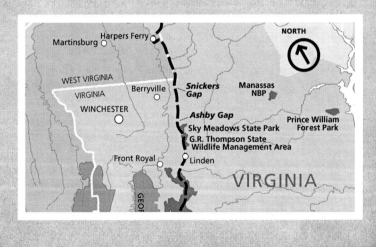

I saw Greg on the trail a few days later. He was happy. His new plan was to hike to Harpers Ferry and leave the trail there.

In March, less than a week before I left on my hike, I went on a day hike with some friends. We went to Sky Meadows State Park in Virginia and hiked up a trail with blue blazes to the AT. Standing on the AT, looking south, I remember being anxious.

So many things were unknown. I wondered about things that seem trivial now. I wondered how I was going to get from the airport to the start of the trail. I wondered what the trail would be like and how my body would react to the daily hiking. I was anxious about how I would re-supply on the trail. Would the campstores on the trail have what I needed? Would my mail-drops get lost in the mail?

My friends and I took a break on a bench at the side of the trail. A couple of white blazes where visible in both directions. Facing north I saw a sign that said "Harpers Ferry 38 Miles" That seemed like a long way. Never mind that Springer Mountain was 965 miles to the south. I was too excited about starting the trail soon and too anxious about tiny details to be overwhelmed with how many miles I would have to hike to get back to that point.

We all started our hike back to the car. I lingered a bit imagining the moment two months later when I would see the "Harpers Ferry 38 Miles" sign again.

While hiking the AT in Shenandoah National Park, I realized that I could be at Sky Meadows on a Saturday if I planned my days right. During the week, I sent out some emails letting friends know where I would be and asked if they wanted to hike a bit of the trail with me.

GUEST HIKERS

Today my friends Pete, Steve, and Gary repeated the hike we took in March from Sky Meadows State Park to the AT. When I hiked at Sky Meadows in March, I remember feeling anxious and uncertain. Now, months later, all uncertainty is gone and the trail is a source of comfort.

Pete, Steve, Gary and I continued to hike north on the AT for a few miles. They are all fans of the outdoors, all more so than me. Pete is of "Pete and Michaela" who are sending me my mail-drops. They are avid kayakers but also like hiking and biking. Gary and I run together most Sundays. I met him and his wife through my running club, but they spend many vacations hiking and backpacking. Steve is now a serious triathlete but spent six months living out of his car out West while bouncing from park to park hiking and otherwise enjoying the outdoors.

It was a nice morning to be out. We hiked north towards Ashby Gap before they had to head back. It was a nice way to start my day.

After my guests turned around, the trail got muddy once again and the day heated up. A couple of early afternoon thunderstorms cooled things off.

Today I entered a section called the Roller Coaster. There are many ups and downs by Virginia standards, but no worse than Georgia. Partway through, I came upon a man on the trail named Out of Breath, who hiked the AT in 1998. It was raining, but he provided trail magic and had several umbrellas in stock. He also had various sodas, bananas and cookies. It was a nice break during the afternoon downpour.

In the middle of the Roller Coaster is Bears Den Hostel. It is an old stone house owned by the Appalachian Trail Conservancy. The hostel was full of hikers and was a relaxing place to be.

Guest hikers Pete, Steve, and Gary

The key to hiking the AT is a light pack. Less weight on your back means more comfort while hiking, but it also means less comfort in camp. Every hiker determines their ratio of comfort in camp to comfort while hiking. That ratio is expressed in how many pounds your pack weighs.

There is no limit on pack weight. If you want, you can cook with an iron frying pan and eat your dinner while watching a portable TV. A practical limit reveals itself while hiking up and down the hills in Georgia those first few days. While hiking, people carefully weigh the benefits of the items they are carrying on their back.

First to go would be the portable TV and the accompanying batteries. That feels better, but then, after the introspection gained by climbing a few more mountains, you realize that you don't really need the maps of where you have been and you throw those out. Then you consider that you really don't need the pages out of the *Companion* for places you've already been, and you carefully cut those pages out of it and toss them.

A few mountains later, you realize that those maps have some pretty wide margins, and you carefully trim them off. A few hills after that you realize that the AT is pretty well marked, and you don't need maps at all, and out they go.

Next you realize that your pack has an awful lot of dangling straps on it and soon the ones that you don't use are cut off. Any excess on the straps you do use is also thrown away.

By Virginia, about one fourth of the way into the trail, most thru-hikers are identified as much by their fashion as their smell. The standard thru-hiker uniform is all synthetic clothing, running shoes, trekking poles and one of a handful of packs that are known for their light weight.

I was like most people and packed light from the outset and simply fine-tuned my gear along the way. Some people though, didn't get the pre-trail memo and they, after time, became legendary on the trail.

There was one guy who started the trail not only carrying a full bottle of fuel, but also two, one-gallon containers of extra fuel while he hiked. That might realistically be enough fuel to hike the entire length of the trail without refueling, which might be what he had planned.

Buffalo Bobby was also one of those legends. In North Carolina, several hikers told me he started hiking the trail with an 80-pound pack. According to the rumor, Bobby bought all new gear at Neels Gap (30 miles into the trail).

I met Buffalo Bobby at Bears Den. He is an easy going eccentric genius who runs at a slightly different pace than the rest of us. Expecting that the legend had been dramatically exaggerated, I asked him if it was true. Surprisingly, it wasn't exaggerated much. He started with 70 pounds. He was able to give or trade away most of his heavy gear. He traded his three-person tent for a one-person tent with a section hiker who had a dog. At Neels Gap, 30 miles into the hike he bought the lighter weight version of a few things. By the time I met him, he had all of the standard lightweight gear including running shoes.

BOB

For what it is worth; I hiked across the 1,000-mile mark today. There is no actual mark, but the Data Book *tells me I've gone over 1,000 miles.*

1,000 miles is a weird milestone. Like a birthday, nothing seemed to change.

I also entered Maryland this afternoon. Five states done. At least that milestone means something to people who know where Maryland is.

Yesterday I did eight whole miles. Actually that is not true, I did 7.9 miles. I went from Bears Den to the Blackburn Trail Center (another very nice hostel). It was a relaxing day, and it felt like a zero day.

The caretakers at Blackburn served dinner, which 10 of us enjoyed. An eight-mile day is even more relaxing when you don't have to cook.

Today I felt like I had my trail legs back. It helped that the 12 miles to Harpers Ferry were easy going. I made good time.

I thought I was almost to Harpers Ferry when I met three hikers coming the other direction. They were most likely grandfather, father, and young son. We talked a bit. One of the adults complained about the ups and downs since Harpers Ferry, and estimated it was 1.5 miles away from where we stood talking. Dang, I thought I was almost there.

They asked me if I thought they could make it to Blackburn, about 12 miles away. I, of course, knew nothing about them or their hiking so I had no idea if they could make it. I diplomatically shrugged and said "Sure."

We went our different directions. Three minutes later I was looking at Harpers Ferry. I wondered about those three guys, I don't think they'll make it.

In Harpers Ferry I visited the Appalachian Trail Conservancy headquarters and had my picture taken, which seems to be the thing to do.

I walked to the outfitter in town with Buffalo Bobby, who I ended up spending most of the day with. We talked about what we use to motivate ourselves to get up the trail. "Greg" came up (he had met Greg earlier). It was an interesting discussion.

For the most part I don't need motivation, the trail seems like the right place to be, and hiking seems like the right thing to be doing. I do look forward to town stops, and when I'm in town I look forward to getting back on the trail, odd. Buffalo Bobby looks to hostels for motivation. In fact, as we walked out of Harpers Ferry, he was headed toward a nearby hostel.

After a good lunch, Buffalo Bobby and I continued our conversation as we left Harper's Ferry. As we walked down the C&O Canal towpath, I told Buffalo Bobby about a camping trip I took about six months before I started hiking the AT.

I went on a short camping trip to try out some of my new lightweight gear. Some was newly bought, like my hammock; some was newly made, like my stove. For my shakedown trip I chose to ride my bike from Pittsburgh to Washington D.C. and camp along the way.

During my bike trip, I rode on the C&O Canal towpath, and rode by Harpers Ferry. For three miles the AT follows the C&O Canal. When I rolled past Harpers Ferry on my bike, I thought about my AT hike.

I wondered if I would have the courage to start my hike. I wondered if I would enjoy the hike and if I would make it to Harpers Ferry. I remember visualizing myself walking across the bridge that crosses the Potomac River and down the spiral staircase that leads to the canal's towpath. What would the hike be like? Would I like it? Would I make it this far?

While I biked the next few miles I was caught up in the fact that I might actually be walking those miles six months later as part of an epic hike.

Walking where I had biked brought those thoughts back. I had started, I had made it to Harper's Ferry and now, as I walked with Buffalo Bobby, I was walking that bit of the canal that I envisioned myself walking months before. So many questions about the AT had been answered, and all the anxiety was gone.

Buffalo Bobby was quiet while I told him my story. As we walked he stared down at the pea gravel surface of the canal's towpath. I sensed that he shared my sentimental mood. He thoughtfully lifted his gaze from the ground and turned to me and asked "What kind of tires do you use for a trip like that?"

We got to the point where the trail for the hostel split off. I had gotten to know Buffalo Bobby and liked talking to him. I thought about staying at the hostel, but my obsession with making miles pushed me on. With 1,000 miles down, and over 1,000 to go, I was very anxious. The rest of the afternoon I debated if I was okay with only hiking 17 miles that day. It was more than enough, but even after a long lunch in Harpers Ferry, I was in camp with plenty of daylight left.

There was a real temptation to keep walking, but a new pain in my heel told me to just stay put. I looked at the *Data Book* a zillion times to satisfy myself that staying was okay and was not going to ruin my chances of getting to Maine.

Ed Garvey Shelter in Maryland

MISSED LUNCH

Last night I had a deluxe shelter to myself so I decided to stay inside for a change. Then John J. showed up. He was nice to talk to and the two of us divided up the shelter. I had the upper portion and he had the lower. The upper had its own entrance, a real door and even a good place to hang my hammock. That made me happy.

John J. had just bought a book in Harpers Ferry. It was called Being Introverted in an Extroverted World *(or something like that). John J. also designed and made most of his gear. So we had a lot to talk about.*

Today while I was hiking, I had a sharp pain in my heel. I put a little duct tape on it and that seemed to cure it.

While I was walking, someone doing the Maryland Challenge passed me. They were running at a good pace and it looked like it wouldn't be a problem for them. That put me in a good mood. The Maryland Challenge is to hike the 40 miles of the AT that goes through the state of Maryland in a single day. There isn't a West Virginia Challenge; I guess it's too easy since there's only 3.5 miles of the trail in that state. There is a Four State Challenge though, which is to touch four states in one day. You start in Virginia, hike through West Virginia, through Maryland and into Pennsylvania.

A few days ago I heard that Tuba decided to do the Four State Challenge. People who do the Four State Challenge carefully word their accomplishment and say they hiked in four states in one day. This is because the AT follows the Virginia/West Virginia border for 16 miles. Most challengers will start the challenge where the AT finally leaves the Virginia/West Virginia border instead of hiking the 16 miles where they run together. This results in a 43-mile day.

Tuba was an ultra-purist though, at least as far as the Four State Challenge goes, and did not want to enter West Virginia at all until he started the challenge. A problem with that plan is that he did not know for sure if the state line would be marked. To play it safe he stopped where he knew he was in Virginia, a mile or so south of the spot where the trail joins the Virginia/West Virginia border (which turned out to be marked after all). Tuba had to travel almost 60 miles to complete his challenge.

Enough about challenges…

At Crampton's Gap I ran into John J. again. I told him about a great place a few miles up the trail that I heard about where we could eat lunch. He said it sounded good, and we agreed to meet there. I arrived at the restaurant first and found out it is only open for dinner. I left and guessed that John J. would figure things out.

Despite a steady rain and giving John J. some misinformation, I was in a good mood. I stopped at the Washington Monument (there's more than one you know) for lunch. While the obelisk on the Mall in the nation's capital is the most famous monument to the first president of the United States, the town of Boonesboro, Maryland has the distinction of erecting the first monument to Washington in 1827.

I asked the park ranger there for some change for a soda. She gave me change, plus a soda. Very nice. While I ate my lunch (trail mix), we talked. I answered a few of her questions about the trail, and she talked about Civil War history. The area is rich in Civil War history and there are many exhibits near the monument related to the war. This was slightly confusing, considering Washington is famous for his accomplishments in the Revolutionary War.

I spent most of the rest of the day walking. I did 24 easy miles so that I felt like I was making progress. It was odd. Seventeen miles felt like no progress, but 24 miles felt like progress. Of course, I only *need* to do 16 miles a day to be in Maine before Labor Day. Sixteen just doesn't seem like enough.

My new shoes were becoming very painful. In retrospect it's easy to see that the shoes were a problem. While on the trail, I never sat back and truly evaluated my foot problem. I always took it day by day and my foot pain proceeded to get just a little bit worse each day. I was worried about it and wondered how my feet would last and what I would do if they gave out.

As I got closer to the halfway point of the AT, I became overwhelmed. It was the first time it really hit me how long the trail was. I had hiked for two and half months, and I was only halfway. It seemed like a year's worth of things had happened during that time.

If I analyzed it rationally, nothing changed. I was still on track to finish by Labor Day. A week earlier, I looked forward to the trail that was left with eagerness, but something about reaching the halfway point made it seem daunting. The mind is very odd.

While I was on my two-week break from the trail, many of the people I slowly passed during the first two months passed me. In the shelter registers, I would see familiar names of people and knew that they were just ahead. I looked forward to seeing those people again and finding out how their hike was going.

ICE CREAM

I'm in Pennsylvania. Maryland went by quickly. The trail in Maryland and Pennsylvania are the easiest yet. There are rocky sections, but there are also long, smooth, flat sections.

In Pennsylvania there are two slightly smaller shelters instead of one normal sized one. Last night I had a shelter all to myself, so I could put up my hammock inside again. Sheep was in the other shelter where he hung his own hammock. Being able to sleep in my hammock in an empty shelter is far better than the shelter experience I had back in North Carolina, when the shelters were crowded and I had to sleep on the floor.

My feet hurt again today. Some of the pain was sharp, and I'm concerned about this. I think my shoes need more arch support, so I used the rest of my duct tape to add a few layers under the arches and I cut squares out of my already cut-down pack towel and sandwiched them under my arches. That made things a little better.

With about four miles left for the day, I bumped into Pez, Booble, Sweet Ass, Strappy and Tucson. Except for Tucson, I had met everyone before in North Carolina or Tennessee. It was nice to catch up.

I'm with that group now at the Ironmaster's Mansion in Pine Grove Furnace Park. The mansion is now a hostel. It is huge with all the standard mansion features, including a secret room. The caretaker for the hostel said that the mansion was a stop on the underground railroad.

Pine Grove Furnace Park is the halfway point of the AT. The tradition is to eat a half-gallon of ice cream when you get here. The sun was out and heated up my appetite the whole day.

I can eat much larger quantities of food now than I ever could before I started hiking the AT. A half-gallon of ice cream looked like a lot, but I was feeling pretty hungry. Today it wasn't meant to be though. While eating my ice cream, my stomach craved hotdogs, so I ate a few of those and then returned to the ice cream. Still no appetite for ice cream — at least not a half-gallon appetite. No half-gallon club for me. Booble downed his half gallon and received the ceremonial ice cream spoon for his effort.

Pez was Pez, and Strappy was a total babe. I met Strappy briefly at Miss Janet's in Tennessee, but hadn't seen her since. Besides being good looking, Strappy knew how to camp. I don't usually think of someone as being good at camping, but she was. She set up her stuff without any fanfare. She used a tarp and had the rare talent of being able to pick a spot to set it up that didn't turn into a river when it rained.

When Strappy cooked, she casually gathered a few rocks to make an impromptu pot stand. When she was done cooking, she returned the rocks and you'd hardly know she had been there.

Strappy's camping prowess would have gone unnoticed except that she was hiking with Pez, who was the total opposite. The AT was Pez's first camping trip. Even after 1,000 miles, he was just learning how to camp.

When Pez cooked, it caught everyone's attention. For a while his stove used twigs and leaves for fuel. This was a great concept. Weight is important and he could save the weight of the fuel. In practice though, there is a lot of fanning of the fire, accompanied by copious amounts of smoke and floating embers. It was entertaining to watch, as long as you were upwind and had your own food covered.

At Pine Grove Furnace State Park, Pez decided he had enough of the leaf and twig powered stove, so he constructed a stove fueled by alcohol out of some soda cans. The stove was made on the trail and it looked like it.

Pez building a fire for cooking

MY FEET

I'm at Darlington shelter, about 12 miles from Duncannon, Pennsylvania. It's early and raining as usual. A few folks are huddled inside the shelter, some are even in their sleeping bags already. My big dilemma is, should I hike eight miles to the next shelter or stay put?

It's a stupid thing to think about. I'm staying in Duncannon tomorrow, so leaving here tonight won't get me to Maine any faster. It just makes tomorrow's eight miles even shorter. This is what I agonize over when I arrive at a shelter early.

My insole modification seems to work. The sharp pain is gone, and the dull aching pain is much less. I think the arch support I have is the bare minimum, but enough. I also hiked in the thicker of the two pairs of socks I have, although they are wet. They seem to help lessen the pain as well, so now I only have one pair of wet socks to hike in.

The last I saw from Wild Flamingo and Hoser was that they were 11 or so days ahead of me. That's about 220 miles at their pace. It's not likely I will see them again. It's nice to be able to keep tabs on them though through the registers.

Today the trail crossed the Cumberland Valley. It was very flat, as it has been for most of Pennsylvania. Tomorrow I will stay in Duncannon at the Doyle, which is a classic AT spot. Wild Flamingo emailed me from up ahead and said that the Doyle is a good place to stay. I also have a mail-drop waiting for me there.

The only other excitement I have to report is that it's supposed to be sunny tomorrow.

The hike from Pine Grove Furnace to Darlington shelter was one of the muddiest sections yet. There were sections in sloped fields (with good drainage) where normally grassy ground had turned into a bog. In some areas, the trail maintainers put down short boardwalks. Nothing fancy, just some planks attached to logs to keep hikers out of the mud. There was enough water in some sections that the planks were floating.

Soon after I arrived at the Darlington shelter, Pez and Strappy arrived and it was time to cook. It was raining and Pez chose to try out his stove on the floor of the shelter, which was a bit congested with people and their gear. The people in the shelter understood and made a little room on the ledge for Pez to cook and then returned to their books or journal writing.

What the residents of the shelter could not have known, was that this was Pez's initial use of his brand new trail-made stove. The stove lit normally, but soon became a raging fireball. This immediately captured everyone's attention. Pez was unfazed and continued to heat a pot of water over the stove as it occasionally ejected a splatter of flaming alcohol. No damage was done, but not a lot of reading or journal writing was done either.

I found out from a shelter register, that Mr. Ed was three days ahead of me and thought that I might be able to catch him. Mr. Ed covers a lot of ground in a day, so in order to catch up I'd have to hike even more miles than he did. He was somewhere between 60 and 75 miles ahead, so if I did five miles extra each day, it would take me about two weeks to catch up.

Then I read in a register that Mr. Ed was hiking with his mom. The whole day I figured I would be able to make up a few extra miles on them. Not that I thought his mom was a slow poke, but for the most part, people don't get on the trail and start doing 20-mile days.

When I arrived at the next shelter, I eagerly checked the register to see how many days I made up on Mr. Ed and his mom. The register revealed that they hiked 18 miles, the same as me. I was very impressed.

Photographing my reflection in a Duncannon store window

The Doyle Hotel in Duncannon, Pennsylvania

Duncannon

"Because they don't make Triple Fudge."
— Booble, when asked why he got a Double Fudge Yoo-hoo®.

I arrived in Duncannon the next morning. The Doyle Hotel is $17.50 a night for any room (single, double, whatever), no matter how many people stay in it. It used to be a very deluxe hotel, but has become a bit run down. The Doyle has a few residents that rent rooms by the week.

The rates are cheap and it is 100 feet from the AT, so of course hikers flock to it. It also has a bar, although the bar was closed when I arrived. With the bar closed, I went to a nearby pub with Pez, Strappy, Booble and Tucson. When the pub closed, we went to a pizza place.

The next morning, the sun came out. It wasn't just peeking out from behind the clouds, it was out with all of its power. Happy day! My stuff, and the trail, had a chance to dry out. At 9:30 a.m., I was happily sitting on the porch of the Doyle, in the sun, thinking about possibilities for lunch. It didn't look like I'd make the 28-mile day I had planned, and I wouldn't gain on Mr. Ed at all, but I didn't worry. I'd have the rest of the summer to make up those miles.

I expected that the sun would bring out the bugs, so I broke down and bought some bug repellant. The directions on the can said to wash it off as soon as possible after using it. This concerned me and I wasn't sure I should put it on for a week at a time.

I decided to stay in Duncannon for lunch. After a good lunch, I was sure I could do 16 miles out to a spring where I could camp. While relaxing on the porch a bit longer, I decided that I'd be okay with an 11-mile day to the first shelter outside of town. Soon, I entertained the thought of staying another night in town.

Duncannon had some mysterious grip over me and the rest of the hikers I arrived with. It wouldn't let us leave. Somehow, I began to pry the town's grip loose and walked out in the early afternoon. I figured the rest of the people there were sure to stay another night.

SUMMERTIME

I managed to escape Duncannon. I don't know why the town was so hard to leave. Not much was going on there. I think it had to do with the nice day. It felt great to lounge around the porch at the Doyle.

The weather finally matches the season. It is hot, or at least very warm. Tomorrow is supposed to be hot. I'll take hot, humid conditions over the cold rainy days we've been having.

The heat seems to bring out the snakes, and they are moving faster than ever. I almost stepped on one. The snake's poorly chosen escape route went right across the trail, around my legs. He was gone before I could react.

I think I've entered the rocky part of Pennsylvania that I've heard about. It's not bad though, and there is a lot of flat ridge walking also. Where it is rocky, the rocks are rough sedimentary rocks (Kneepad, who has a geology degree, told us that) and they provide good traction. A few sections require a minimal amount of scrambling, which is a nice change of pace.

The shelter tonight is great. It's one of the bigger ones I've seen. It has a loft, porch and an enclosed picnic table. It probably sleeps 25 very comfortably, 50 in a pinch.

I'm in my hammock though. It's hot out and now the cool sleeping hammock is a real advantage.

As I was cooking, people started rolling in. I thought that some or all of them might not be able to escape Duncannon's grasp, but it turns out that everyone from the Doyle is here. Plus, a few more — like Mr. Ed!

I was surprised to see Mr. Ed. I figured with my slack mileage he was way ahead. It turned out that he and his mom got off the trail in Duncannon for a few days. On the one hand, this was a bit of a relief since I was considering doing some really long days to catch him. On the other hand, he was doing 31 miles the next day, so I wasn't sure I could stay with him.

We saw in a register that Wild Flamingo was about 12 days ahead and had a minor foot issue. We also saw that Hoser was two days in front of him but planned to go fast to catch up with some other hikers. There was little chance I'd catch either of them since they were in pursuit mode.

Mr. Ed and I ended up hiking the rest of Pennsylvania together. He was one of the more insightful people I met on the trail, and we talked about how the trail might be changing us. We reflected on simple trail life verses "real life." When compared to trail life, real life is very commercial and materialistic.

On the trail in Pennsylvania there were a few signs that the park services posted to warn hikers about Lyme disease and the West Nile virus. Pennsylvania was a hot spot for both and the signs provided information on what to look for and how to minimize your risk.

Real life had signs too, but they were all advertisements. From the perspective of a thru-hiker, they were advertisements for stuff you cannot use. While hiking in the woods, you are advertising-deprived. There are no ads on the AT, only trees. I saw ads in a fresh way when I took time off from the trail.

Even all the nice shiny stuff in an outfitter seemed too bulky or heavy for a thru-hiker. I remember going into an outfitter in Pennsylvania and realizing that there was nothing there for me to buy. I owned everything I wanted and it all fit into my small backpack.

The exception was food. I would enter a restaurant and feel like asking for "one of everything."

FEET AND BUGS

Today I planned to hike 31 miles to stay with Mr. Ed. The terrain was easy, mostly flat, with only the occasional rock. Thirty one miles means waking up early and walking faster than I normally walk.

I left about 7:30 a.m. I needed every hour of the day to hike 31, so I left before Mr. Ed and Kneepad (who has been with us the last couple of nights).

Only 2.5 miles into the hike, Mr. Ed and Kneepad caught me. That was a bad sign for me. We all hiked on and off together and soon it was clear that my feet didn't want to go 31 miles. Kneepad (who is smarter and wasn't planning on hiking 31 in the first place) and Mr. Ed ended up thinking the same thing.

During the day we had an air show. Several types of military jets flew overhead. The trees made it hard to see the planes, but we could hear them for an hour or so.

Kneepad, Mr. Ed and I are now camped next to a creek and very close to a busy road. We're about 22 miles from where we started this morning — not the 31 miles I anticipated, but much more than the 16 miles I "need" to average.

I was almost famous. I was walking down the trail and saw two ladies hiking toward me. The first thing they asked me was if I was Iron Toothpick. I thought, "Huh??" Being on the trail provided a certain amount of anonymity and that was broken when I heard my name. It turned out that they were friends with the park ranger I met at the Washington Monument in Boonesboro, Maryland.

The bugs were out in full force. We passed signs that said the West Nile virus was active and to try not to be bitten by mosquitoes. They didn't give any advice on how to keep them from biting though.

Everyone had their favorite bug force shield. My scheme was my hammock, which had bug netting over the top. I was also packing a one-pound can of insect repellant that I sprayed on some of my clothes. I was afraid to use it on my skin though.

Kneepad had a beekeeper-like net that he put on before getting into his sleeping bag. The netting protected his head and his bag protected his body. It turned out that in the hot, humid weather, the bug net was a bit warm.

Mr. Ed had a huge bug net that he suspended from his hiking poles to create a 45 cubic foot bug-free zone.

The next day, Kneepad hiked on ahead of us to try and catch his friend Bookworm. With the constant threat of rain gone, Mr. Ed and I decided to just camp wherever we felt like it. This provided much more freedom than limiting ourselves to shelters. Camping randomly meant it was just us. This was no big deal — unless the campsite was haunted.

HAUNTED CAMPSITE

Today was hot, and when it's hot, we don't hike as far as we are used to going. I guess I should have known that the heat would slow me down, but it came as a bit of a surprise.

On the first leg of the hike, I ran out of water about 90 minutes before the water source. Not very smart. When we arrived at the spring we found a pipe with water gushing out.

Mr. Ed didn't always filter or treat his water. Today, I joined the club.

I drank a liter of the cool spring water and filled my water to capacity (three liters) even though the next water source was only four miles away.

The rocks that Pennsylvania is famous for appeared today. We've seen short rocky sections before, but now the rocky sections are almost continuous. The rocks are punishing my feet, although I expected worse. I guess hearing about them for 1,100 miles has prepared me.

The rocky section apparently continues for several more days. We also heard that the trail in New Jersey is actually under water right now and that the water comes up to your knees.

Mr. Ed and I were tired as we entered the last campsite we could reach today. The choices were: Camp there and get eaten by bugs, or hike on and camp at some random place and avoid the bugs for another hour or so.

We filled up with water and were on our way. An hour later we came to a spring. Excellent, we hauled water 3.5 miles to a spring. That's always satisfying.

We surveyed the camping situation, and we both found places to setup for the night. The woods were thin, but I found two trees with soft ground underneath. Mr. Ed scoped out a nice grassy tent pad. We then went to visit the spring to clean up. When we came back, some guy's gigantic car camping tent had materialized in Mr. Ed's perfect spot.

The new guy, I'll call him Jerry, came from a nearby road. He sounds like he comes up here a lot to hang out in the woods.

While Mr. Ed and I were setting up camp in a new spot, Jerry told us a story about how he saw a sasquatch standing right where we were. He also alluded to the fact that he has heard voices and screaming in the woods on previous trips.

We are about 50 yards from the ruins of Fort Dietrich-Snyder. The fort was used in the French and Indian war as a lookout. Jerry seems to think that there was probably a lot of killing here, and that many ghosts remain. Jerry also likes to get high although he smoked in his tent out of consideration for us.

After getting a little high Jerry went to a nearby field to light off fireworks. We followed, more to keep an eye on him than to watch the show. The show was around 10:00 p.m., way past our normal bedtime.

The show was lame. I think Jerry thought he should have gotten more bang for his buck. After the show we followed Jerry back to the campsite.

Tomorrow I plan to get to Port Clinton before the post office closes. It shouldn't be that hard, although Jerry reports that the heat index will be 105 degrees and that they are advising people to stay indoors.

As predicted, the following day was hot. As we hiked, I felt myself heating up, but I knew we were coming up on Port Clinton in a few miles. As we descended from the trail into town, the air became even hotter.

I went to an outfitter to seek refuge from the heat, but they were located on the top floor of an old building and didn't have air conditioning. I was feeling pretty bad and eventually found refuge in an air conditioned bar.

In the bar I found Kneepad who we assumed was well ahead of us. Upon entering town he asked around and learned that Bookworm was in the emergency room in a nearby hospital. He had contracted Lyme disease and most likely hiked out of Duncannon with it. The telltale Lyme disease bulls-eye was on his back and escaped his notice.

The hike between Duncannon and Port Clinton gave the disease time to develop and by the time Bookworm reached Port Clinton he was in very bad shape. It didn't sound good.

When we encountered day hikers in Pennsylvania it seemed that everyone either knew someone who had Lyme disease or they themselves had it.

Lyme disease is spread in two ways. It is spread by adult ticks that are barely visible to the naked eye, and by nymphs (pre-adult ticks) that are just a speck. There are signs on the AT showing the magnified ticks and warning people to constantly check for ticks and remove them promptly. This is an impossible task.

My fear of getting sick fueled my mileage obsession. The sooner I was out of the Lyme disease zone the better.

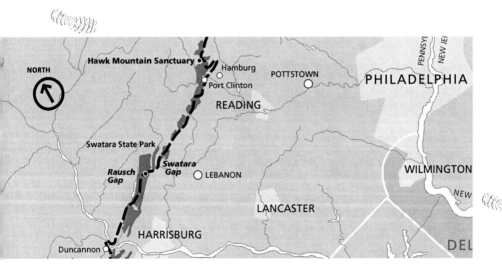

Port Clinton, Pennsylvania

Mr. Ed navigating Pennsylvania's famous rocky terrain

Best Trail Town

PALMERTON, PENNSYLVANIA

Yesterday was hot and the terrain was rocky, just like today, and probably tomorrow. In the middle of the day we stopped at a shelter to beat the heat.

A man maintains the shelter in his backyard. It was a one-room shed, with doors and lights. On the porch of his house is a fridge with cold sodas and ice cream sandwiches. Just the thing for the heat. Mr. Ed and I hung out there for hours.

We actually stayed a bit too long. When we hit the trail again we realized we wouldn't arrive at the next campsite until after dark. So we stopped short of the campsite and called it a day.

Mr. Ed's morning routine takes a couple of hours. This means we don't start hiking until 8:30 a.m. or so, which on hot days means we waste an hour or two of cooler hiking weather. By stopping short he would be able to go to bed early and wake up early and possibly break out of the cycle of 8:30 a.m. start times.

This morning we left at 7:30 a.m., 7:29 to be exact. Our early start worked well and even with the rocks we made good progress before the heat of the day kicked in.

We stopped at a shelter to eat and fill up with water. The spring had a snake in it. The snake was about half in the spring and half out, with its head submerged. I considered not using the spring, but I figured I could safely get my water from a pool just upstream and avoid contamination.

Getting water from some springs is a little tricky. You don't want to stand in them and contaminate the water. So you perch yourself, just so, usually straddling the small pool. This gives you easier access to the deepest part of the water. So I balanced myself in the usual position and touched part of the snake. The snake was alive!

Back at the shelter I kicked back and told Mr. Ed about the spring. Another thru-hiker joined us, and we talked about what was coming up. I lay back on the shelter floor, and noticed another snake coiled up in the rafters. So I got up and let them know there was a snake as I stepped out of the shelter. They both looked up and just shrugged it off. The snake looked like it was pretty happy where it was.

The Data Book *revealed that there was a bowling alley in the next town, which was Slatington. Even though it would be a short day, Mr. Ed and I decided bowling would be fun.*

But now, instead of stopping in Slatington, we are in Palmerton, Pennsylvania, the friendliest trail town so far. We are staying for free in the basement of the old police precinct.

We ended up in Palmerton entirely by accident. The *Data Book* mentioned that Slatington had a bowling alley, so we were all set to stay there. On the road to Slatington, there was a car rental place. We borrowed their phone and called the hostel in Slatington. Nobody was there. While thinking about what to do next we talked to the guys working at the car rental office. They told us that Palmerton was close and that hikers could stay in the old police precinct for free. I mentioned that we were set on bowling and wanted to go to Slatington.

The guy behind the counter informed us that the bowling alley in Slatington was a mile outside of town, and that it was closed. Mr. Ed and I looked at each other. No bowling alley meant we would keep on hiking. Then the guy mentioned that Palmerton had a bowling alley and that it was in town. He gave us directions and we were off.

On the very outskirts of town we passed some houses. A couple of people were working in their yards. Mr. Ed whispered to me "I wonder if that guy would give us a ride?" As he said this, the guy, Derick, yelled down and asked us if we wanted a ride. Amazing. Derick found his keys, got his Bronco and picked us up. What a nice guy.

On the way into town, Derick gave us the tour and explained where everything was. He also explained the procedure for staying in the jailhouse.

The procedure for staying at the jailhouse was to check in with the police. They took your name and presumably checked to see if you were wanted for anything. While checking in, I made some joke that didn't go over well. The police in Palmerton are pretty serious, which I guess is what you want in your town's police officers.

The jailhouse was actually an ex-jailhouse. The basement had no hint of any bars and was just a big open space. The local Boy Scouts built a half-dozen bunk beds for hikers. The Girl Scouts put together care packages containing a toothbrush, toothpaste and shampoo.

The icing on the cake was that the shower flowed like a fire hose. Maybe it was the shower they used to de-lice prisoners. When it was on full blast, spraying down on your head, you could feel additional pressure on the bottom of your feet. It was also as hot as you wanted it.

The shower was just a tiled area on one side of the bathroom. No stall or curtain for those prisoners. Opposite the shower was an open window and through the window you could hear the choir from the church next door.

The town looked like a movie set for a generic small town. In addition to the friendly vibe, the town layout was ideal. A laundry facility was across the street from the jailhouse and the ice cream shop was a couple of doors down from that. Everyone we met went out of their way to make us feel welcome.

We hadn't seen many other thru-hikers in recent days. I think everyone was spread out. It was just Mr. Ed and me in the basement until a southbounder (Just Jim) showed up.

Just Jim had all kinds of information on the trail ahead. I found out that the Pennsylvania rocks that I thought might be over soon continued into New Jersey, probably two or three more days. Just hearing that news caused my feet to hurt.

Just Jim clued us into some good places to stay that aren't in the *Data Book*. In exchange we told him about the Doyle in Duncannon.

After dinner Mr. Ed and I went bowling.

On the way back from bowling we got to walk through Palmerton's nightlife. The nightlife consisted of kids cruising the strip in their cars and hanging out in front of the convenience store. It was like being in a 1950s movie, except that the cars were modern.

The next morning we hit the diner for a big breakfast. After eating, we went back to the jail to pack our stuff. Back at the jail we met Grizzly who had just rolled in. Grizzly liked to talk. At first I thought I was in a normal conversation. Then I realized that no matter what I said or asked, his conversation kept on going in the same direction like a big heavy locomotive. It sounded like a conversation, but I was more of a spectator. Mr. Ed escaped and made some phone calls upstairs. I took a nap. Grizzly kept talking to me even as I napped.

The lottery was over $200 million, and Mr. Ed and I were feeling pretty lucky. We each bought some tickets on the way out of town. How cool would it be to win $200 million while walking the AT? As we began to walk toward the trail Derick spotted us. He made a U-turn and pulled over and soon we were piled into his Bronco, capping off a great town stop.

Barren mountains surround Palmerton. There is a factory in Palmerton that does something with zinc. Years ago the exhaust from the factory spread zinc onto the surrounding mountains. Every spec of vegetation vanished. I read about this in the *Companion,* but seeing it first hand was impressive.

Derick told us more about it as he drove us back to the trail. The factory cleaned up its emissions over 30 years ago, but the vegetation on the mountains was just beginning to return. Crews were planting various hearty plants to bring some life back to the barren mountains.

This barren landscape made the AT around Palmerton very exposed. A big change from the green tunnel we usually walked through. Mr. Ed and I ended up hitting the trail at about 1:00 p.m. We climbed out of the gap, with no shade on the hottest part of a sunny day. It turned out that the polluted area was not actually that large, and we walked out of the exposed ridge and into the shade in an hour or so.

We rolled into the Leroy Smith shelter in the late afternoon to find two people handing out Snickers, and Sprite. Very cool. Pez and Strappy were also there.

GOODBYE PENNSYLVANIA

This morning we hiked 20 miles. Mr. Ed, who usually leaves late, was ready to go early. We were walking at 6:30 a.m. The walk has been terrible for the past few days because of the heat. Bugs added to the frustration. Mosquitoes were landing on us while we were on the move. Despite the oppressing sun and humidity, Mr. Ed chose to wear his rain gear to protect himself from the bugs.

After a rocky walk, we reached Delaware Water Gap, Pennsylvania and easily found the church hostel. I lay down on the couch and remained there for a few hours while my feet throbbed, reminding me how much I have abused them on Pennsylvania's rocky terrain.

Right now I'm at the Church of the Mountain Hostel. It is 0.2 miles by trail from the I-80 bridge that takes you to New Jersey. I'll be out of Pennsylvania today, something I've increasingly been looking forward to for the past few days.

I usually look forward to being in a new state, but this time I'm happy to be done with Pennsylvania. For the last few days the rocks have been getting worse, and my feet are totally abused. All of my nagging foot issues are gone and have been replaced with large volumes of general achiness. This is the result of stepping on sharp angled rocks that tenderize your feet.

The majority of the trail through the state is very pleasant and goes through a nice variety of woods and fields. It's only that final good-bye from Pennsylvania that makes you dislike the state. I've enjoyed almost every day of this trip, even the endless rainy days. I did not enjoy the last few days of Pennsylvania. If the whole trail was rocky like the last few days, I don't think the AT would be nearly as popular.

Gadget was staying at the Church of the Mountain Hostel. I met him when I first started the trail in Georgia. He delivered the "Gadget lecture" on Springer Mountain. He was spending the summer as the Ridge Runner for a section of trail in northeastern Pennsylvania.

The Fourth of July was coming up, so I asked Gadget if any good towns were on the horizon. I wanted some cool July Fourth experience. Ideally, I would have ended up in Palmerton on July Fourth. Celebrating the holiday in a small town would have been great, and Palmerton seemed like just the right sized town.

Gadget lent me his atlas, and I checked out the statistics on towns I would be near around the Fourth of July. Both Gadget and the atlas indicated that there was nothing promising. Mr. Ed was leaving the trail for a bit in New Jersey. I was more than a little bummed that the holiday would be just another day on the trail.

NOT SO SECRET SHELTER

Yesterday, Mr. Ed got another early start and left Pennsylvania to hike with his cousin. I slept in since I was only going to hike 10 miles. I roamed around Delaware Water Gap for a bit and finally headed out late.

I got to the Mohican Center, where I planned to stay. I was just in time for lunch. There were some youth groups there and it looked like it would be a loud evening. I decided to hike another seven miles and camp.

After reaching the camping spot, I cooked, but then felt like hiking some more. I ended up hiking another seven miles. When I'm hiking alone I tend to put in bigger miles, the same thing happened in lower Pennsylvania.

I spent the night with zillions of mosquitoes. The place I chose to stay was near a swamp. The air was thick with insects and the cumulative noise of their buzzing filled the woods with a loud hum. I had already eaten dinner, so I threw up my hammock as fast as I could and got in. Once inside I was safe from the mosquitoes, but could still hear their constant din.

This morning I packed in record time to minimize the number of mosquito bites. I started hiking without eating breakfast. There was a bakery at the next road crossing. I hiked to it and waited for it to open. The bakery is famous among hikers for being closed on Tuesdays. But it is Wednesday so I got a sandwich (the place is a deli too). I also bought some day-old rolls, which I'm guessing were two days old since they were closed yesterday.

Wild Flamingo had previously told me about the "Secret" shelter in New Jersey. It sounded interesting, and I planned on stopping there, assuming I could find it. It is not marked, and is not in my Data Book. The road to the shelter is just like any other road. Wild Flamingo said I would know it by a sign there that said: "Water 500 Yards."

Just before reaching the sign I found a small note nailed to the south side of a tree. The note said: "NOBOs you really want some of this water!"

For over a week Mr. Ed and I had only seen one or two people at the shelters. Since splitting from Mr. Ed, I have only seen one other thru-hiker. Walking into the secret shelter I found 10.

The secret is definitely out. The shelter was actually several nice cabins with running water (hot and cold), and showers. Very deluxe. The cabins were located in a field. The place was well kept, but there was no sign of the owner.

People were making plans to celebrate the Fourth of July. Some folks were going to camp at a spot where they thought they would be able to see the fireworks in New York City. They seemed like a cool enough group, and I ended up hiking with them. No small town parades, no Fourth of July fair, watching fireworks from a distance would have to do.

FOURTH OF JULY

It was very buggy yesterday. New Jersey is known for its bugs, and the locals say this year is worse than ever. Even in the middle of the day the mosquitoes form a small cloud that stalks me while I'm hiking. When I stop, it's a nightmare. They land as fast as you can swat them away. So I don't stop. But they still manage to bite me when I'm on the move. They bite everywhere; on my neck, my arms, even my fingers and knuckles. I burn half my calories hiking and the other half swatting. My bug repellant only helps a little.

The trail came to a point where it followed a mile of boardwalk through a marsh with tall grass. There was a bench along the boardwalk, and strangely, in the middle of the swamp there weren't any bugs. I finally stopped for a break and soon Big Paw and Wolfman joined me. After a snack we walked two miles to a farm along the trail that had ice cream and soda.

Wolfman had a bulls eye mark show up on his skin, so he thinks he might have Lyme disease. He and Big Paw headed into Vernon, New Jersey to find a doctor.

This morning I left camp late. My plan was to hike to Mombasa High Point to camp and watch fireworks over New York City. Right around the New York/New Jersey border, I caught up with Tooth Fairy, Flanders, Bree L.T.C. (Like the Cheese), Uno and Plato. They were lounging around on a rocky outcrop taking a break. It was there that we met the German family.

The Germans were day hiking. They stopped and chatted with us a little as we lounged around on the rocks eating energy bars or trail mix, or whatever else we had in stock. They asked us all the usual questions and took pictures of us. They seemed friendly enough and mentioned that they had a house on a lake and invited us to come down for a swim.

I don't know what the others were thinking, but I was wavering. I was planning on hiking 18 miles and felt I didn't really have time to hike to some lake, especially since they said it was a half hour hike away. I felt this would blow the whole day. Taking a break sounded nice, but making miles sounded better.

The lake idea sounded good to most everyone else though, so I decided to follow. I figured I could probably still get 18 miles in, I'd just have to walk really fast when I got back to the trail.

We followed the Germans down the side of the mountain, wondering what we'd find. After leaving the AT, the hike didn't follow a clear trail. I started second guessing my decision to follow. Did I really want to do this?

At the bottom of the hill we entered a nice neighborhood. They did indeed have a place on the lake and they also had nice shade trees. We all set down our gear and enjoyed the shade. It was a hot day, and I can't convey how good it felt to lay down and relax on cool grass. Then one of the Germans, Christina, came out of the house with an armful of beers. Things were good.

After a bit more lounging, we all jumped in the lake and spent some time swimming and hanging out on their dock. Then another girl came out of the house with a big bowl of watermelon. On the trail everything is either warm, or if you cook it, hot. While sitting on the dock at the edge of the lake, eating cold watermelon, I decided that this excursion was worth any miles I would miss.

From the dock we saw activity around their grill. Were they having a cookout? Were we invited? This was too good to be true. While we pondered the possibility of a cookout, Barbara, another German, gathered our clothes and put them in their washing machine.

Soon we were all eating hot dogs, hamburgers, and salad. The conversation and food were excellent. After the cookout we enjoyed the various lounge chairs and hammocks they had around their yard. We all napped. Slowly, with every rock of the hammock, I decided I'd be okay hiking a little bit less that day.

After a nap came dessert — in the form of an ice cream cake. We couldn't believe the incredible trail magic we stumbled across. That morning I wondered what kind of Fourth of July I'd have. I figured I would hike all day and camp someplace that had a view of the fireworks. I never imagined a cookout.

Finally, our stomachs were full and our time was up. After a few pictures with our generous hosts, we all piled into two cars for a ride back to the trail. We thanked the Germans for making the day truly special. They told us about a good spot to watch the fireworks, so we hiked a few slow miles to the spot that appeared to be the place.

The fireworks didn't start until way after our normal bedtime. All of us managed to stay up to watch what must have been the longest fireworks display I've ever seen. I took a nap during the middle and Plato went to bed before it ended. The fireworks capped off a great day.

I can't thank the German family enough. They welcomed six smelly strangers to their home without hesitation. They were truly generous with their time and their food. A photo they mailed me after I returned home is my favorite photograph of the entire trip. It's a group shot that includes five hikers I only knew a few days and a German family I knew for only a few hours. It reminds me of one of the best afternoons of the trip.

Our Fourth of July trail magic became a minor legend. Later, while in Vermont, I overheard another hiker telling everyone about the ice cream cake and swimming and . . . .

FRIENDLY NEW YORK FOLKS

New Yorkers are pretty friendly. In addition to the Germans, I met two more friendly people in New York today.

The Data Book *said there is a deli at West Mombasha Road. A sign at the road crossing confirmed this. It was a half mile off the trail, but it was lunchtime and I had some extra time.*

After walking more than half a mile, I asked a man where the deli was. He said it was just over the hill but it was closed for the weekend. That made me a little sad. Images of ice cream sandwiches instantly evaporated in the 95 percent humidity.

The only thing left to do was to walk back to the trail and have gorp for lunch. While walking back, another man pulled over in his car and asked me if I had any luck at the deli. I told him it was closed. He said there was another deli three and half miles down the road and offered me a ride.

I loaded my gear in his minivan and off we went to the deli. He even waited for me while I got my sandwich and soda. I normally would have loaded up on all kinds of junk food, but he was waiting, so I limited myself to just a sub.

While driving back to the trail in the minivan, I talked with the man about the AT. He said he was planning a local hike, but that his wife wasn't on board because of the "Bear Mountain incident." Huh?? I'm hiking over Bear Mountain tomorrow, so I asked him to tell me about it.

It turned out that some time ago, he told his wife that he was going to hike to Bear Mountain and asked her to pick him up in the afternoon. What he didn't realize was that it was 23 miles from his house to Bear Mountain. Not a short hike.

I didn't get all the details, but I think it involved his wife waiting around for hours for him, which was the crux of the "incident." Fortunately, this was no threat to me.

Then he dropped me off at the trail. Very cool — deli-to-trail service. It made my day.

Later in the day it turned hot. I guess it wasn't so much hot as it was humid. In any case, it was uncomfortable. There also wasn't much water on this section of the AT, which meant two things. One, I had to carry a lot of water and two, the water I had was warm.

I met a couple along the trail who gave me a liter of cold water. It was the best. The girl also offered me half her sandwich, which was turkey — my favorite. I like New York.

Wolfman, the hiker I met a few days before who thought he had Lyme disease, was prescribed antibiotics. The doctor he saw in Vernon told him to get plenty of rest and to stay out of the sun. He didn't really follow that advice and continued hiking.

Another hiker, Plato, who I spent the Fourth of July with, was also sick. He visited a doctor the week before. The doctor didn't know what was wrong with him and he also prescribed antibiotics. Plato took five days off the trail, but couldn't stand being cooped up, so he started hiking again. He still wasn't feeling well though, and hiked a short day the next day.

Getting sick on the trail was my number one concern. Other minor concerns I had were where to get fuel for my stove, where to re-supply and where to get a new *Companion* (mine was missing the last four states on the AT, part of my clever plan to save weight).

NO MONKS

Today's plan was to hike to a monastery that takes in hikers and feeds them dinner. During the day I had images of monks in robes with shaved heads. I wouldn't mind a shaved head, I figured I would see if they offered haircuts.

On the way, the trail climbed over Bear Mountain and into the town of Bear Mountain, New York. It's more of a park than a town. I was planning to eat big. I asked a man picking up trash where to eat, and he pointed me to the Bear Mountain Inn.

What he didn't tell me was that the inn didn't open for a couple of hours. Very funny, ha ha ha. I asked the lady at the Inn where I could get a burger and she told me that they sell food near the merry-go-round in the park.

I found the concession tent near the merry-go-round, set down my pack and thought about how many burgers I felt like. I'd start with two. But there was a catch. The lady working there said that they couldn't sell burgers until they set up the cash register. I asked her what time they would be set up. She didn't know. It was one of those frustrating situations where they could sell burgers (the food was there and ready, I had exact change, etc.), but wouldn't.

I left the park burgerless. I have plenty of gorp and wanted to get to the monastery for my haircut, so I hiked on.

On the way I saw a rattlesnake, turtles, huge frogs, an otter and all kinds of salamanders. This was because the AT goes right through a zoo. It's not a huge zoo, but it had a sampling of the animals in the region.

I crossed the Hudson River and hiked some more. Around 2:00 p.m. I arrived at the trail that goes to the monastery. There are friendly signs posted that let hikers know how to get to the ball field.

As I walked I wondered why a monastery has a ball field. It turns out they have all kinds of stuff, including a sewage treatment plant. The place is huge.

The monastery turned out to be a total let down. It was actually a friary and the men there wear normal clothes (even on Sunday) and have normal hair (so no haircut for me). Their building looks like an office building complete with loading docks in back.

The procedure for dinner was to walk up to the building and wait at the loading dock. They then escort you to the dining room.

Dinner was a buffet, but they brought the food to me and the other hikers I ate with, which was very nice. They even had a table reserved for hikers at the far end of the cafeteria. They had meatloaf, which made me happy.

After dinner I lounged around a pavilion near the ball field with some other hikers. Medicine Man has a new tent and since he is partially blind, I read the directions for the tent while he put it up. It was a very exciting evening.

Hiking In Waldies®

DURING MY BREAK FROM THE TRAIL, Wild Flamingo and I bought identical trail shoes. They were extremely hip and futuristic looking, but I bought them anyway.

A few weeks later, I received an email from Wild Flamingo (who was ahead of me about 12 days). He told me that he was taking a zero day because his feet had been soaked for days.

I thought that was odd. The shoes were not that comfortable, and were a source of a few foot problems for me, but their redeeming quality was that they were waterproof. Not just kind of waterproof, but bombproof waterproof that also allows your feet to breathe.

I knew this because I tested this feature every day while crossing the swollen creeks and mud bogs in New Jersey. While others tiptoed around mucky areas, making the trail ever so slightly wider, I walked down the center of the trail.

My favorite feature of the shoes was that they gave me the ability to stand in the streams that crossed the trail. The water would cool the shoes down and make my feet feel good. At first, the chill made me think the shoes were leaking, but they always stayed dry inside.

So when I heard Wild Flamingo's wet feet story, I didn't say anything. I figured he wasn't using the shoes right.

TWO TOES UP

We've had a two-week streak of very enjoyable sunny rainless days. That streak ended yesterday afternoon. After picking up some food from a deli, it started to rain.

The rain was heavy and when it rains hard the trail turns into a shallow stream. My shoes look a little worn these days, and are splitting slightly in a few more areas, but I wasn't worried since they're waterproof. But something was different this time. That cool sensation in my shoes was also squishy. It took about 30 seconds for both shoes to become fully saturated. I think I now understand Wild Flamingo's problem.

This morning the shoes were still wet and heavy. It was sunny out, but my dry pair of socks quickly became damp in my wet shoes. As I walked the 10 or so miles to another deli, I thought about how the shoes' only redeeming quality had vanished. Now I have shoes that cause all kinds of weirdo foot pains AND they get wet inside.

The deli visit went like they normally do. I got ice cream, a soda and a meatball sub. I put my Waldies on and read a New York Post *that Night Runner had left on the picnic table.*

Finally, I figured I should start hiking again. I wasn't looking forward to walking in wet shoes with wet socks, so I tried to dry my socks out by wearing them in my Waldies (which have a lot of ventilation) for the half-mile walk back to the trail.

It was very hot out and by the time I reached the trail my socks were dry. I saw that the trail continued across some pastures. It looked like smooth terrain, so I figured I'd keep going and switch to the wet shoes when the trail demanded it.

My feet gave the hiking in Waldies experiment two big toes up. They handled a few stream crossings, a few rocky sections, and some ups and downs. I ended up hiking in them the rest of the day. Since there are no trash cans on the trail I also lugged around three pounds of wet stinky useless shoes.

While I'm tempted to keep hiking in Waldies, I'm going to get new shoes tomorrow when I get to Kent, Connecticut. I walked 26 miles today, the last 16 in the Waldies and my feet feel great for once. There were a few tricky sections where I should have had shoes, but they prevailed. I hike much slower in them and ended up doing a little night hiking since I misjudged how long it would take to get to the next campsite (in Connecticut you can't just camp anywhere).

So far, all of my miles in Connecticut — eight of them — were hiked in Waldies. My feet want me to hike the three miles to Kent in them too. After Kent there are only 40 miles to go in Connecticut. I'm considering hiking all of Connecticut in them, just for a change of pace.

The next day, I hiked three miles into Kent in my Waldies, visited an outfitter, bought new shoes, and had breakfast with Night Runner.

Looking for shoes, I vowed to get New Balance, since that is what I wore for the first 500 miles of the trail and they treated me well. However, the only outfitter in town didn't have much of a shoe selection, so I bought Salomons.

A week or so before getting to Connecticut, my mom put me in touch with my cousins, the Boccuzzis, who live in Connecticut. The original plan was to hike a bit of the trail with them. My mileage obsession, combined with the fact that I reached Kent in the middle of the week, caused me to abandon the idea of hiking with them. Instead we agreed to meet for dinner.

Kent is one of the more expensive towns on the AT. A church there allows hikers to stay in their recreation room, but there are no showers. Most people who stay at the church use a solar shower that an art store in town set up for hikers. It was overcast out, and I wasn't looking forward to the cold shower.

I hadn't had a real shower since Pennsylvania, and had not done laundry since Palmerton. I've gotten used to the smell, but with all of the hot humid days, I'm sure I was pretty stinky. I didn't think that a cold shower was going to cut the smell enough.

In a rare splurge, I got a hotel room. By the afternoon I was clean, my clothes were clean, I had gotten a deluxe hair cut (Kent only has deluxe) and my beard was trimmed. I was now suitable for visitors. I spent the rest of the afternoon watching the Tour de France (team time trial) on TV.

The Boccuzzis showed up at my hotel room as planned. I looked at my watch and they were right on time, to the second, which was remarkable since my watch was wrong.

It had been a few years since I saw my cousins, so we caught up and of course talked about hiking the trail. After a very nice dinner, we walked around Kent and got some ice cream. It was a very pleasant and relaxing evening.

Appalachian Trail Railroad Station. The train to NYC actually stops at this station.

WALDIES CONNECTICUT CHALLENGE

I hung out in Kent this morning and finally left town around noon. On the way out I stopped by a bakery to load my pack with fresh cookies and a deli sandwich.

I declined the Waldie Connecticut challenge and walked out of Kent in my new shoes. I was seriously considering hiking in Waldies, but it seemed pretty dumb to carry around a brand new pair of trail runners and hike in camping shoes.

The trail north of Kent got a little more rugged, making my decision to hike in shoes a good one.

The AT only goes through 51 miles of Connecticut. Initially, I wondered why there wasn't a Connecticut challenge. Now I know why. Connecticut is rugged and has a lot more ups and downs than the trail from Virginia through New York.

I'm glad that things have become more interesting. The AT was getting a bit boring lately. Hence, I was considering the Waldie Connecticut challenge to make things more exciting.

In the afternoon I caught up with Medicine Man. He wasn't sure where he was and was glad to see me. I wasn't really sure where I was either since it had been a while since I had passed a recognizable landmark.

We hiked together and he talked about acupuncture, chiropractic, yoga, tai-chi, and natural herbs. He is the Medicine Man after all. He told me he has "worked on" a few hikers and fixes various aches and pains.

I mentioned some slight numbness I consistently have on the outside of my left thigh. He mentioned the names of some vertebrae and said he could work on me. I think I'm going to pass on the adjustment, but I also think I might change how my pack is riding.

We rolled into camp late (7:45 p.m.). The shelter was packed. The people were very nice and said they could make more room. I passed and told them I'd set up my hammock.

A guy in the back of the shelter mentioned it was going to rain tonight. I laughed at him and made some comment about him being a section hiker and what does rain have to do with setting up my hammock outside. As if I'm some camping god.

I found two perfect trees and set my hammock up while thinking about my rude section hiker comment. I ate my deli sandwich (chicken salad with sprouts) and a few cookies.

The shelter was over capacity even without me, and soon Ultreya set up his hammock to escape the packed shelter.

Venus and Duke asked me how the Fife 'n Drum Inn was (where I stayed while I was in Kent). I said it was great, especially the copious amounts of hot water in the shower. They weren't amused, I think they were miffed that I didn't invite them in for a shower.

I seemed to be alienating everyone, except for Medicine Man who was very grateful for having me as a hiking partner today.

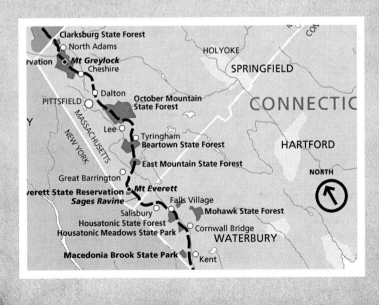

Buying Salomons shoes turned out to be a good decision. After several days my feet started feeling really good. After a week I didn't give my shoes or feet any thought at all. I was able to hike easier and faster and even ran at times. I had once again found shoe nirvana and would hike the remaining 600 miles of the AT in the shoes I bought in Kent.

The next day, I could see Lime Rock racetrack from the ridge where I was walking. It was a road course and it looked like a few cars were practicing. I hoped that the AT would get closer to the track, or go right by it, but it stayed on the ridge and eventually the track was out of sight.

The trail also followed a wheel-chair accessible nature trail, went by a power plant and past a waterfall. The waterfall was not that spectacular since most of its water was diverted to the power plant.

For whatever reason, I felt full of purpose. This was crazy considering my only purpose was to hike to Maine. Taking the summer off to hike from Georgia to Maine was pretty useless. Hiking the AT didn't help anyone, didn't further any causes, and didn't offer me anything tangible. So it's odd that while on a useless self-created adventure I felt so satisfied. I wasn't sure what to make of it.

I was definitely enjoying the second half of the AT more than the first. I'm sure it was the sum of many things: there was less rain, the terrain was more interesting and there were fewer people. I think a large part of the euphoric feeling came from accumulated time on my Appalachian retreat.

My biggest worry was getting hurt or sick. One day, as I was walking, I thought, "That rock looks slick, maybe I should avoid it." The thought was more of a daydream and didn't register with the part of my brain that was in charge of my legs and feet. I stepped directly on the slippery looking rock and confirmed that yes, it was slick. I half-fell. For the next hour I thought about how bad it would be to get hurt, just when things were getting good.

Laurel Ridge Campsite in Massachusetts

SILENCE

Last night I camped just over the Massachusetts state line.

Today I stopped by The Corn Crib for a snack. It's a fruit stand off of a major road that is only 0.1 miles from the AT.

I sat in the gazebo at The Corn Crib eating ice cream, a banana, and a Snapple. A lot of cars sped by, and there I was, in the middle of a Saturday, by myself, snacking.

Normally, if I had stopped to buy some snacks, I think I would go directly home. Sitting around eating seemed a bit odd when there was an audience.

It was another long day to get to the East Mountain Retreat Center. Wild Flamingo recommended it, so I built it into my schedule at the last minute. It's a nice place, and I'll zero here to give Mr. Ed a chance to catch up. Lately, I write my plans for the next day in the registers for Mr. Ed who is about one and a half days back.

The registers allow me to see who is just ahead. One guy even writes a short comic strip in them that I see from time to time. If I see a name I recognize, I usually have a few days before I'll see that person. During that time I'll remember a few things about them. By the time I see them, I usually know where I met them and who else was there when we met.

This aspect of the registers is great. I'm normally slow to remember people. If I meet someone, and they say that they know me, I usually remember their name or other facts hours later.

I caught up to Phoenix and his dog Cody. I met them just outside of Erwin, Tennessee. Phoenix didn't remember me at first, so I mentioned where I saw him and his dog, and that One Side was there. I always feel like a real people person mentioning all of these things about the last time we met.

I finally made it to the East Mountain Retreat Center, which is almost two miles off of the trail. There is a sign as you go up the half-mile long driveway to the retreat warning hikers to be silent.

The folks that go to the retreat center go for the peace and quiet. They stay for the weekend and don't talk to each other. These people don't want to talk and don't want to hear others talking. Hearing the crunching of shoes as a hiker walks up the gravel driveway seems to be acceptable, as is the sound of a pizza delivery car driving up. (Whew!)

The grounds are nice and have various benches and gazebos that look over the valley. There are a lot of places to relax and be quiet.

At the back of the retreat is a really nice hiker hostel with laundry facilities, a phone and a shower.

I talked to the lady who runs the retreat and she said that hikers aren't allowed to roam the grounds. So it looks like my zero day will be spent on the sofa and since nobody is around it will be silent.

The trail is a little more rugged these days, and I think I'm going to adjust my mileage. I did the math and I only need to average 13.5 miles a day to finish by Labor Day.

Tomorrow is a big day. Not because of the mileage, but because I pick up a mail-drop. This mail-drop not only has the normal food, but also has a new toothbrush! Pete and Michaela usually include a picture and a note, which is really what I'm looking forward to.

Riverman ended up staying at the retreat center with me. He was a section hiker and lived in Reston, Virginia (where I live) for 16 years. He was resuming a thru-hike he started a few years before.

I planned to sleep in on my rare zero day. As Riverman left, he let a cat in, which foiled my plans to sleep in. He decided to sleep on top of me, which was fine. Then he started kneading the blankets, and I discovered that he had a complete set of claws. I'm famous for not liking needles, but my dislike extends to anything sharp and includes cat claws. I couldn't sleep with the cat claws in such close proximity.

Around this time in my hike, a euphoric feeling began to build. It would come and go, but overall it got stronger. When I first started the AT, I was happy because I was finally on the trail. For months I had read about and planned my hike and was happy to have finally started.

The next source of happiness was realizing that I didn't have to work. I like my career, but spending every day out in the woods was a welcome change of pace. At home if I wanted to go hiking on quality trails I would have to commute to the trail. During my hike there was no commute.

Around the time I was in Massachusetts, I began to think about wants and needs. The reality is that what a person needs is practically nothing. Food, water, shelter and companionship pretty much sum up all of my needs. Between the contents of my backpack and the other hikers on the trail, I had all of that. Life, as I lived before the trail, seemed ridiculously complicated, and for no legitimate reason. The later portion of the hike clarified for me the difference between wants and needs.

I knew these things before the trail. If there was a multiple-choice test before the trail I would have known the difference between wants and needs. I would have easily scored 100 percent. My knowledge of wants versus needs was in a useless part of my mind. It was knowledge that I had, but did not apply. Being removed from the normal routine of life put things in a different light.

GOOSE POND CABIN

After I started hiking today, I realized that I was going to arrive at Tyringham around noon. I remembered that the post office had odd hours, so I looked them up. It turned out the post office was closed from 12:00– 4:00 p.m. Because of poor planning I was going to have to wait for four hours before the post office re-opened so I could get my mail-drop.

I decided to run. The terrain was as good as it gets on the AT. Easy hills and soft dirt footing with a lot of bounce. I got to the road before 11:00 a.m., and with a lift from a friendly farmer, I was at the post office with plenty of time to spare.

Tyringham is very nice. It's like the town on the "Newhart" show. The post office takes up half of a small stone building and the other half is the town library. There is not much else, not even a soda machine.

It was a nice day, and I sorted out my loot on the lawn beside the post office. As people walked by to get their mail they smiled and asked how I was doing. One guy came over, sat with me and chatted. We talked about the town and the Tyringham Cobble, which is what they call the rocky outcrops that overlook the valley. It looked like a very pleasant place to live.

After Tyringham, I only had to hike eight miles to get to a cabin where I planned to stay. I had plenty of time and took it slow. It was a nice relaxing afternoon.

I caught up to Riverman just before reaching Goose Pond Cabin. We walked in together around 4:00 p.m. The cabin is pretty nice. I wouldn't call it deluxe, but it is located in a beautiful spot next to Goose Pond. The cabin has a bunkroom, propane lights and a stove. There's a canoe that visitors can take to explore the pond. There is no water source near the cabin, so the caretaker uses the canoe to cross the pond where there is a spring.

At the cabin I met Little Mermaid. He and I went out in the canoe to check out the lake. I have no idea how he got his trail name, but it certainly seemed like an unlikely fit for him. We talked about all of the cool stuff coming up (Long Trail, the White Mountains, Maine) and how it must be sad for the southbounders who are leaving it all for the New York–New Jersey–Pennsylvania stretch.

Upper Goose Pond, Massachusetts

THE MAGIC WORD

Last night a southbounder named Bluegrasshopper told me about a guy in Dalton who lets hikers stay at his house. Bluegrasshopper said to go to the gas station and mention this guy's name.

I went to the gas station and the attendant approached me and asked me if I needed any help. Odd, I figured with my backpack and hiking poles, I must look like a hiker, and if hikers always come there it should be obvious. Maybe I was at the wrong place. I hesitantly mentioned the name Bluegrasshopper gave me. That was the magic word. The attendant disappeared to make a phone call. A moment later the attendant was back. He said someone would be by shortly to pick me up.

Little Mermaid and Medicine Man were already there. I showered and borrowed some clothes that were way too big for me. Our host then took us for pasta and ice cream.

The guy who owns this place a super generous — he invites hikers into his house and doesn't even charge a fee or ask for a donation. He is very approachable. I later learned that when he isn't hosting hikers he plays in a rock band that has been together since high school. While we were there he played a little guitar.

Right now Medicine Man is giving the owner some kind of therapy. A combination of chiro and massage. During dinner Little Mermaid ate too much and looked sick. Medicine Man did a little of his healing and Little Mermaid is mostly better. So Medicine Man is living up to his name tonight.

Tomorrow we'll probably hike a bit and have the owner of this place pick us up. It's easier for him to drop us off down the trail so that we hike back, but Little Mermaid and I are both the types that want to hike the entire trail northbound. The other dilemma is slack packing. I'm going to take my pack, but leave most of my full food bag here (I think). Little Mermaid feels the same way about all the miles being northbound and slack packing, so at least I'm not the only freak.

Keith and Anna finishing the "Vermont 100"

I'm Not Crazy, You Are

WHILE IN DALTON, I received an email from a friend who told me that another friend, Anna, was running a race in Vermont that weekend. After some emails and phone calls she agreed to pick me up in Vermont on the way to the race.

So the night I entered Vermont, Anna, with her husband Jim and their son Michael, picked me up in Bennington for a little vacation from the trail.

The race was the Vermont 100 Mile Endurance Run. The "Vermont 100" is a 100-mile race in and around Woodstock, Vermont. The race is for both people and horses. It started as a horse race and 15 years ago they began to allow people to run the same course.

This year they rounded up 300 competitors. I talked to several of them while milling about the registration area. It came up that I was on a break from hiking the AT. A guy who was waiting to register for a 100-mile race rolled his eyes when I told him how long the AT was. He called me crazy. I'm thinking running 100 miles straight is totally nuts, but I was outnumbered. Plus, the AT is just 22, 100-milers. The rumor was that Pete Palmer was racing the Vermont 100 Mile Endurance Run that year. In 1999 Pete Palmer hiked the entire length of the AT in 49 days.

All of the runners lined up at the starting line at 4:00 a.m. The start/finish area was on a very nice horse farm. Before the start they had a small fireworks display, while a pianist played *Chariots of Fire* — a very odd scene at 4:00 a.m.

For the next 30 hours I watched the race and helped Anna however I could. Mostly this amounted to filling water bottles and other things I could do to allow Anna time to relax as best she could at aid stations. I also volunteered to pace her from 10:00 p.m. to 3:00 a.m.

At home, Anna is an active ultra-runner and encourages others to join the ultra ranks if they seem interested. Her motto is: "If you can run a marathon you can run a 50 miler." By itself that is a ridiculous statement. A marathon is 26.2 miles, 50 is almost twice that. It doesn't make sense, but by the time you have talked with Anna for a while it makes total sense.

Sometime in those early morning hours I got to see a side of ultras that she doesn't advertise much. Any attraction I had to running a 50 or 100-mile race was neutralized between the hours of 1:00 a.m. and 3:00 a.m. If you have a fascination with how people deal with a lack of sleep and tremendous pain, help pace someone through a 100-miler. You get a front row seat to their misery.

Around the time I started pacing Anna, she caught up to Keith, who was also from Reston. Keith, Anna and I ran and walked through the night. Early in the morning, Mars and the Moon marked the passage of time as they tracked across the sky.

Before the sun came up, my shift ended, and I easily fell asleep. I managed to wake from my nap shortly before Anna and Keith went on to finish.

Anna and Jim dropped me off on the trail mid-day. Jim hiked with me for a half mile to get a taste of the trail. I hiked another mile to the first shelter, set up my hammock and slept to recover from my "zero days."

Anna taking a break during the "Vermont 100"

BUSY TRAIL

Today was a good hiking day. It looked like it would rain the whole day, but waited until after I was at a shelter.

In the middle of the day I took a break and discovered a ton of kids out for a hike. It was actually about 10 kids, but it sounded like a lot more. I found out that they were planning on using the next shelter, which happened to be where I was headed.

While hiking I decided I would cook and go at the next shelter. I'd get to see the kids come into camp, and also get to see the expressions on the faces of the thru-hikers already there when they arrived. Then I would go.

The forecast was for thunderstorms and they sounded like they were approaching fast. The pending storm made me decide to stay in the shelter, despite the loud campers that were bound to show up. I staked out my place in the shelter and started cooking.

The rain held off while I cooked, but started as a few other thru-hikers rolled in. Everyone opted for the shelter and soon it was almost full.

The group of kids eventually arrived as the rain really started to pour. Our dinner entertainment was watching them set up a huge tarp over a side trail. They were pretty quick and all of the kids and their packs were under the huge tarp in short order. The drainage wasn't so good and soon a few of them were working on a trench to allow the water that was pooling up to escape.

The rain stopped and the sun came out. It was still early, so I packed up my stuff and hiked on a little.

Now I'm camped about two miles from the top of Stratton Mountain. I'm just off the trail, not in any official campsite. Some call it stealth camping, but I'm not that stealthy tonight. My food bag is hanging right above the trail, and there is an arrow I made out of sticks reminding me which way to hike down the trail tomorrow morning.

The forecast is for more thunderstorms tonight and it sounds like the forecast is going to be right.

It stormed most of the night, just like the good old days. While I was eating breakfast there were thunderstorms in the area, which wasn't good since I was about to climb a tall mountain. But, as I climbed the mountain the storms ended and the view from the top was clear.

The hike was uneventful. I missed a shelter which threw me off. I felt lost, but a day hiker answered a few questions and it turned out that I was right in front of Prospect Rocks, one of the better views in Vermont so far. I stayed there for a little while to dry my stuff and ate the very last of my food, Ramen and some instant breakfast.

I got to the road to Manchester at about 3:00 p.m. I hate hitchhiking, but it was five miles. There were loads of cars. After a few minutes it appeared that there would not be an instant hitch. I started to walk in, and soon a couple from Florida picked me up. Twenty minutes after leaving the trail I was in front of the Price Chopper (grocery store) and an outfitter.

Prospect Rocks in Vermont

LIVE AND LEARN

My plan was to re-supply in Manchester and hitchhike out so I could hike a few more miles. I was all set to go when I bumped into Wolfman.

Wolfman seems to be over his bout with Lyme disease. He mentioned that he and Grinder were staying in town. So I decided to stay. I figured we would see a movie or do something fun.

Since I've been at the motel, Wolfman and Grinder have been sleeping. The only movies playing in town are "Pirates of the Caribbean" and "Legally Blonde 2."

Oh well, live and learn. I have four days of food, so I can avoid towns until Woodstock, Vermont, and hopefully that will be a short stop.

On the plus side, Manchester has a Ben & Jerry's.

Hitching a ride back to the trail from Manchester Center, Vermont

Journal Entry
July 24

VERMONT WEATHER

The weather in Vermont is wacky. There is a saying that I've heard from a few people up here: "If you don't like the weather, just wait a minute." They are exaggerating of course, the wait is more like forty minutes.

Today we had rain, sun, cold rain, and thunder. But not just one of each. It started out rainy and overcast. Then the sun came out, then a little while later the rain started again. In the middle of the day it was hot and humid. The afternoon alternated several times between sunny skies and thunder/rain. Now the rain has stopped, but it's chilly and foggy.

After a while I stopped putting on and taking off my rain gear.

Now I'm at Cooper Lodge near the top of Killington. The "lodge" is a damp stone shelter that has windows that don't close. It is a very chilly 60 degrees, and you can see wisps of clouds blowing through the lodge. The name sounded cool, but the place isn't.

The next morning I planned to go to the top of Killington. There is a gondola for mountain bikers and hikers can take it down to the resort town below. That was the plan, but the weather was terrible.

I left the lodge with my long underwear top, a fleece and my hat. It had been a while since I hiked in my fleece. A few people said they saw moose, so I was on the lookout for them. The woods were mostly pine in the higher altitudes and the footing was very cushy.

LONG LONG TRAIL

Today I reached "Maine Junction." Maine Junction is the point where the Long Trail and the AT split. The Long Trail continues north for another 165 miles to Canada, the AT goes east. Now that I am off the Long Trail it might be a little less crowded, although AT hikers are probably half of the traffic at the moment. I'm sure the Long Trail hikers are just as glad to pass Maine Junction.

The trail goes through a campsite, and I rested at the park office for a couple of hours. It was sunny, so I dried most of my stuff while I ate and read my email.

After my lengthy break I continued on. The trail had a steep climb that wasn't in the Data Book. *Once I was on the ridge I heard thunder. In Vermont, this of course means nothing. I got sprinkled on and arrived at the shelter just as the thunder stopped.*

I only did 16 miles and was in camp very early. It felt a little odd, but the next shelter was 10 miles away, and I didn't feel like hiking 26 miles total. I spent the afternoon eating and watching the traditional camp entertainment-people cooking their food. Four Feet was trying out a new stove. I think he and Pisces designed it. So we had extra special entertainment that evening since it's always fun watching a new stove design make its debut.

Mighty Mouse and The Bishop arrived. They were going to cook-and-go and camp along the side of the trail somewhere. I decided to tag along to get a few more miles in and make the day seem more satisfying.

I have no idea where we are camped now, maybe two or three miles past the shelter.

Things are good. I went through a couple of days where I was in a funk and was miserable (mostly because of the weather) but that seems to have passed. New Hampshire is just around the corner...

SECOND WHAT?

I hiked over many hills today. The trail surface was smooth and cushy though, so it made for a nice workout. I just cruised up and down Vermont's Green Mountains.

It was sunny and several of the hilltops were cleared of trees, so I could see for miles. This was one of my top 10 hiking days so far.

The trail passed near Woodstock, where the Vermont 100 Endurance Run took place. I crossed several familiar sounding roads, but never saw anything that I recognized. Some of the Vermont 100 markers were still up, so I did see where the AT crossed the course.

One of the entries in a shelter register mentioned something about yellow jackets near the second sugar ??? I couldn't really make out what it said, but I thought I'd figure it out when the time came.

After leaving the shelter, I walked through a forest that was mostly pine. I noticed that the trees were growing in neat rows. It seemed strange, looking down rows of tall straight pine trees. About a half hour later, I saw many trees of a different type growing together. The trees had a bunch of plastic tubing strung around them. I stopped and inspected one. The tubes weren't attached to anything; they were just wrapped around the tree.

I walked on and came to another group of trees with more tubing around them. Then I got stung. Suddenly, it all came together. Keith mentioned during the Vermont 100 that tubing is sometimes used to harvest the sap from Maple trees. I figured that the tubes were for that purpose and the register must have said, "second sugar GROVE." None of that mattered of course, I simply took off running. I got away with one sting.

Later in the day, I arrived in West Hartford, Vermont. The *Data Book* said to ask at a nearby store for a place to stay. According to the register in the store, many people have been stung lately by bees. I ordered a couple of sandwiches and asked about a place to stay.

The man working at the store pointed me to Ronnie's. On his recommendation, I bought Ronnie a dozen of his favorite beers and headed toward his house.

Ronnie's wife was in the yard. She pointed me to a cabin and took the beers. I'm not sure if Ronnie saw any of them.

The next morning, after breakfast at a snack bar in town, I walked an easy 10 miles to Hanover, New Hampshire. I was tired and took it easy. While walking I met a southbounder who gave me the scoop on where to stay for free in Hanover.

I met another southbounder after arriving in town. He seemed a little weird, but he was on his way somewhere. A few minutes later he came running up behind me and started walking with me.

I stopped by the Dartmouth Outing Club (DOC). It was open, but nobody was there. The *Companion* said to stop by the DOC to find out where to stay. I had an idea of where to stay; I just didn't know how to get there. The weird guy thought he knew where to go and walked out expecting me to follow. When I didn't, he came back to get me.

I don't know what to do in such cases. When I first saw him he was Mr. Who-Knows-Exactly-Where-He-Was-Going. But then he turned up at the DOC lost. Without getting any additional information he took off like he knew where everything was. So I didn't think he had any clue, plus the guy was weird. Not dangerous weird, but the weird that you don't want tagging along while you are asking strangers for directions.

From what the first southbounder told me, it appeared there were two places to stay. Both were fraternity houses. One place took in everyone that showed up. The southbounder said it was dirty and that there was a fight there the night before. The other place only took in four people and was clean. I opted for the cleaner place of course since the whole idea of staying in town was to get clean.

I stopped by the town information booth and got directions. I met Frantic on the way and we walked over. The weird guy was already there. Luckily they had just enough room for us.

HANOVER, NEW HAMPSHIRE

I'm doing laundry in the basement of one of the dorms at Dartmouth. I can't imagine what the students think of some guy that hasn't showered in over a week, sitting in their lounge in a rain suit.

One girl asked me where the bathroom was. I'm guessing she's new to the school and probably doesn't know about thru-hikers. So probably thinks a homeless guy snuck in to do laundry, which I guess is true.

After my clothes dry and I shower, I plan to walk around town and visit the other fraternity house that takes in hikers to see what I'm missing.

Did I mention that I'm in New Hampshire? I'm both happy and sad about it. On one hand I'm making progress, on the other hand there are only two states left.

During the afternoon I explored Hanover. I also found the other fraternity house. The house could not have been more different from where I stayed. The clean house was a modern apartment building. The other house looked like the set from the movie *Animal House*. Picture the fraternity house in *Animal House*. Now imagine that house after 25 years of neglect. I stayed in some pretty sketchy places on my hike, but the "other" fraternity house was by far the worst. The basement was dark and full of mattresses and other miscellaneous junk. Hikers that stayed there slept in their sleeping bags so they had some protection from whatever grunge had built up since Dr. Seuss went to school there.

I used the public library to catch up on email and to read journals to see how others were doing on the trail. Hoser and Wild Flamingo were about a week away from finishing. I found out that Windtalker left the trail around the half-way point. The last time I saw her she was very upbeat and seemed to have everything it took to finish the AT, or any other challenge. I was surprised to see that she had left, but I hadn't talked to her since Trail Days, which seemed like a lifetime ago.

While roaming around town I met 2-Step and Fast Feet. I met 2-Step before, in May, when Hoser, Wild Flamingo and I gave her a ride to Trail Days. We went out to dinner at an Indian restaurant in town and followed that up with Ben & Jerry's ice cream.

The trail has two distinct personalities in New Hampshire. The first 50 miles are very Vermont-like, easy hills with good footing. The last 100 miles are the White Mountains.

View from the Presidential Range

No Picnic in the White Mountains

I HAD HEARD ABOUT the White Mountains of New Hampshire since Georgia. To get a fresh start into the Whites, I hiked a short day to Glencliff. I arrived at the "Hikers Welcome" hostel around 10:00 a.m., where I relaxed and ate for the rest of the day. I took another short day only 50 miles before in Hanover, so I felt I was ready for the Whites.

In Glencliff the post office was part of the postmaster's house. It was conveniently located across the street from the hostel, and only half a mile from the trail. While the postmaster was looking around for one of my last mail-drops, I noticed a stack of letters addressed General Delivery. The letter on top was for Windtalker. It was a bit odd seeing her letter knowing that she would not be picking it up.

After my hike I found out why Windtalker wouldn't be picking her letter up. Over the summer her Peace Corps assignment came through. She was assigned to a village in the Fiji Islands.

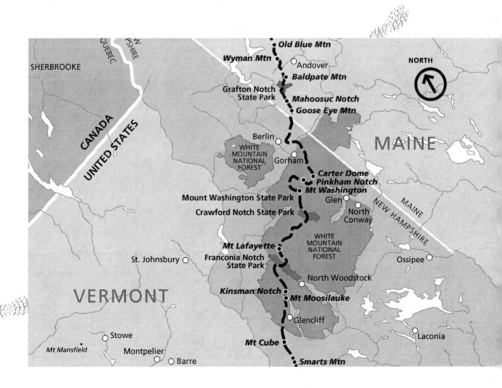

SLOW MILES

Today was rough, both mentally and physically. The day started well with a climb up Mt. Moosilauke. It was an uninterrupted 3,500-foot climb. The footing was good and the climbing was very easy going.

Mt. Moosilauke is the first time the trail goes above the tree line. The weather was good and the views were great, definitely worth the climb.

Then the going got tough. The descent down Moosilauke was slow. It was 2,000 feet over large smooth slabs of rock. There was very poor footing and nothing to grab onto. In some places, if you slipped you would slide 30 feet down to the base of the slab you were walking on. I took it slow and all went well. Part of the descent was next to a series of waterfalls, which made a beautiful backdrop to the trail.

Once at the bottom, I only had seven miles to hike to the shelter where I planned to camp. It was noon, and it was shaping up to be an easy day.

Those seven miles took the longest of any seven on the AT. The trail didn't go up or down too steeply and wasn't particularly hard, but it was slow. There were many rocks and roots. Occasionally, I encountered a section that required a bit of rock scrambling. Not the terrain you make good time on.

On the upside, I met Sherlock and Slick. I had seen both of them before, but got to spend some time with them today. They were good guys to talk to after a frustrating day. We got along well and they were relaxed and funny. Laughing made me feel better.

The forecast says that tomorrow the nice weather will move out, which is a bummer since I'll be entering the Presidential range. It looks like I'll be in the Whites for a long time though, so I'm sure the weather will clear up during my sloth-like traverse of the area.

While I knew the terrain would be tough in the White Mountains, I got depressed as I realized how slow I was going. I began to wonder if I would ever make it out of the Whites.

Contributing to my mood was the fact that my hammock required trees. Since the trail went above the tree line, I couldn't just camp anywhere I wanted. So I needed to think for once, to avoid walking late in the day in a slow stretch with no shelters or trees. If I had my maps, I would have known where the trail went above the tree line, but I sent them home months earlier to save weight.

Most days I had a vague idea of where I'd camp. I might change my mind during the day, but I at least knew I could get to a certain point where I could spend the night. In the White Mountains it was more random. I had to figure things out as I went.

The White Mountains are very popular and there were many day hikers and groups around. Not a real big problem, but at times the trail was congested. I saw day hikers and wondered why I felt I couldn't get anywhere. After all, they were hiking around without a problem.

The biggest issue I had in the Whites was the footing. Every club that maintains the trail has a philosophy for how it should be done and sometimes you can sense when you are in new territory.

For example, in Georgia the trail adamantly follows the mountain ridge and goes over every mountaintop, no matter how insignificant. In Tennessee, the trail is easily graded and only visits the tops of mountains that have unusually good views.

Most clubs make minor relocations to the AT every few years to give the ground a break. This allows the ground to recover before foot and water erosion make a scar on the land. This also means that most of the time you are walking on a fairly fresh trail.

The Whites contain the oldest trails on the AT. These trails existed long before Earl Shaffer first thru-hiked in 1948. Some trails in the White Mountains are over 100 years old.

The people responsible for maintaining the AT in the White Mountains don't believe in trail relocation and the trails are in poor shape because of it. The trail has literally become a channel cut into the forest floor down to rock that was originally smoothed by ancient glaciers. At some points the forest floor is chest high and you walk in a deep trench. The smooth solid rock makes the footing very poor, especially when wet. While going down some particularly slabby parts, you have to reach out for trees and roots on the side of the trail to keep your balance. I found the Whites tough because they require concentration.

Much of the AT has very good footing, and you can let your mind wander while your legs and feet are on autopilot. Not so in the Whites. After a few days, I was tired and worn out, both physically and mentally.

One day while feeling completely exhausted, I encountered a family hiking the other direction. The youngest daughter was maybe eight years old and was bouncing happily along, completely decked out in Barbie® pink (including bulky pink rubber boots). It was like watching a movie. Were these people on the same trail as me? They made it look so easy.

For no real reason, I planned to hike the Whites straight through, without leaving the trail to stay in nearby towns. I planned on bringing enough food for the 100-mile traverse. However, it was clear the first night I camped in the Whites that I was going to run out of food. My stomach demanded two dinners and my slower pace would cause me to take longer than I had planned.

I had heard about the system of huts that the Appalachian Mountain Club operates in the White Mountains. The huts are huge and have enough bunks to sleep 50-100 hikers. They came to my rescue.

The huts in the Whites were similar to the hut system in Europe. People hiked up to them (they are not accessible by road) and either day hiked from one, or hiked hut to hut. Unlike in Europe, however, each had individual bunks. They also cost $70 a night, which included breakfast and dinner but no shower or laundry facilities.

After months of living on the cheap with fellow thru-hikers, I was in a thrifty state. Camping along the AT is free with the exception of the White Mountains. My thriftiness compelled me to get through the Whites spending as little as possible.

Fortunately, thru-hikers have a special deal at the huts. As a thru-hiker I could work-for-stay. Officially, you have to be one of the first two thru-hikers to arrive each day to get work-for-stay, but the hut staff is compassionate toward thru-hikers and can always use an extra hand. In exchange for cleaning the dishes, sweeping the floors, or cleaning bunkrooms, you can stay for free and eat leftovers after paying guests are done with their meals.

Mizpah Spring Hut

HUTS

Last night I visited a hut one mile and 1,000 vertical feet (down) off the trail. I figured I was a shoe-in for work-for-stay. No thru-hiker would climb down 1,000 feet off of the trail.

When I arrived there were already two thru-hikers. Normally this isn't a problem; the crews at the huts can usually use some extra help. Today there was a substitute crew, and they weren't hip to having extra help for dishes.

So I was grouchy. I had just walked way off the trail and was stuck. It was late and rainy which made me even crankier. It's the risk I took.

It didn't help that one of the "thru" hikers just got on the trail yesterday, and the other guy was obviously a section hiker. The section hiker told me he had been there since 10:00 a.m. to get his spot.

So I chose to pay at the hut instead of hike back up to the ridge, at night, in the rain. Because I paid, I was treated like a normal guest. That meant I ate with the other guests which turned out to be a good thing. I spoke with a few people about the hiking they had done in the Whites. We talked about thru-hiking of course, and I got the normal questions. I met two ladies from Pennsylvania that I had met on the ridge and we talked about hiking and outdoor stuff until late into the night.

I consider myself shy and even after meeting so many people on the trail, I was happy that I had the courage to strike up conversations with complete strangers. While others were thinking about how bad I smelled, I was secretly happy to be socializing.

At breakfast I decided to give the ice-breaking thing another try. Being conscious of it put me on unsteady ground, but soon everyone was chatting and having a good time. Then the substitute staff injected themselves.

The substitute staff was in their 50s and 60s. They constantly reminded us that they were a guest staff. I don't think they wanted all of the guests to think that they normally worked at the hut for a living. To drive home the point, they completely interrupted the numerous breakfast conversations for a game. The game was: "Guess what I do for a living."

One by one we got to hear options for each member of the staff, and after voting we heard the answers. Excellent! In my opinion, most of them had rather uninteresting bureaucratic jobs. After you heard their job title you still wondered what they actually did.

I left right after breakfast. It was raining and most of the guests were not in a hurry to get out, so I had the trail to myself. The going was slow, normal for the Whites. It took me about five hours to hike the seven miles to the next hut.

At the next hut I enjoyed all-you-can-eat-leftovers for a buck. It was early so I decided to continue on the trail, maybe camp, maybe make it to the next hut, I'd let the trail decide.

The trail climbed up in altitude, and the weather cleared. I got some nice views of where I had walked earlier in the day.

The going was easy, for the Whites, and I made it to the next hut in time to score a work-for-stay. I was the third thru-hiker, but there was a normal crew and I was in.

Right now I'm in Zealand Falls Hut, about a third of the way through the Whites. The dining room is full of day/weekend hikers who have reserved a bunk for the night. One guy is borrowing the hut's guitar, and he plays really well. He and two others are singing, but it is that soft, self-conscious singing people do when they aren't confident of the words. They look like they are planning on a late night which wouldn't be a big deal except that they are in the common room, where Cue Ball, Radio and I are sleeping tonight.

I became a bit cranky in the Whites. Slow terrain, lots of people and few camping options brought out the worst in a hiker running a calorie deficit.

Most of the time in the Whites my choices for camping were spaced apart by either 7 miles or 14 miles. I found 7 miles was too short, but 14 miles was too long for the Whites. To compound the problem, if you do a work-for-stay you get a late start, and if you plan on getting another work-for-stay, you need to get in before 5:30 p.m. in order to work. This makes for a short, frustrating day over slow terrain.

I pushed myself hard through the Whites. I was afraid I was falling behind schedule— a schedule that didn't exist. After a week I was exhausted. The huts provided some much needed warm meals, but I just could not eat enough to make up for the calories I was burning during the day. My calorie deficit was taking its toll.

Mount Washington is famous for its bad weather. Over a hundred years ago, an observatory was built on top of the mountain to measure just how bad the weather actually is there. In 1934, surface winds were measured at 231 miles an hour, the highest on record anywhere in the world. On most days the summit is fogged in.

There is a road to the observatory on Mount Washington. In addition to the observatory, there is a museum, a post office and a food court. I never would have guessed that Mount Washington was a tourist destination, but when I arrived it was packed with people. The weather was not extreme the day I passed through, just foggy and a bit windy. My clothes quickly became damp from the blowing fog, and I was cold when I arrived.

I stopped in the building with the food court and found a locker room downstairs where a few other hikers were lounging. I bought a couple of slices of pizza for lunch and hoped they would warm me up. Even the air inside the building was damp and cold.

The fog thickened while I was lunching, and it made the trail slightly more challenging to follow. Mount Washington, along with most of the Presidential range (which is part of the White Mountains), is above the tree line. The trail is more of a route across a rocky landscape than the well-worn dirt path I was used to mindlessly following.

On the opposite side of the mountain from the road, there was a cog railway. The trail ran along the tracks for a little while. The rumor was that it's a thru-hiker tradition to moon the train as it goes by. I'm not really the mooning type, but even if I were, it would have been in vain. The train passed by, probably within 25 feet, and I could just barely make it out through the fog. If the train was silent, I wouldn't have known it was there.

MEDICINE MAN

I remember looking forward to the White Mountains because I heard they were both beautiful and challenging but now that I'm here, it really stinks. The thing I like about the AT is its simplicity. Much of that is absent in the Whites.

The Whites are challenging, which is good. The views are nice when it's not foggy. But the Whites have made me realize that I didn't come out here for the challenging terrain or the great views, I came out here to relax and meditate for a few months. I hope to have a chance to return to that before long.

I'm at the end of the Whites now, in my last hut (Carter Notch Hut). Tomorrow, depending on the terrain, I should be out of the Whites and will probably hike 15 miles and stay in Gorham, New Hampshire. I'm looking forward to a shower and doing laundry.

Today, while climbing Wildcat Mountain, thunderstorms started to close in. I always get a bit anxious when there is lightening around, and my anxiety was at its maximum. While climbing the mountain I saw Medicine Man. He assured me that I was on the last bit of slippery slow terrain and that great things awaited me ahead in Maine. Very gentle, very encouraging.

I think I imagined it though. The trail was muddy in sections, and the only (or last) prints in the mud were from a different brand of shoes than Medicine Man wears. Plus, Medicine Man is hiking northbound toward Katahdin, and today I saw him headed southbound. Odd, I'm eager to check his web site to see where he was today.

Cabins at Carter Notch Hut

Medicine Man was right. I was soon at the top of Wildcat and could see into Maine. The trail through Maine would prove to be the best of any state. With the Whites behind me I thought I would be able to make good time. I predicted I would finish in less than two weeks, on August 17.

I started hiking the 15 miles into Gorham. On the way I met Jump'n, who was also headed into town. After a bit of a wait for a hitch we were in town and eventually stumbled onto the Barn.

The Barn was a hostel and it was packed with hikers. In the Whites I wondered where everybody was and it turned out that many of them were at the Barn recovering. Everyone complained about the Whites and the weather. Sharing my misery made me feel a little better.

Everyone was looking forward to Maine. What we did not know at the time was that the first part of Maine was tougher than the Whites.

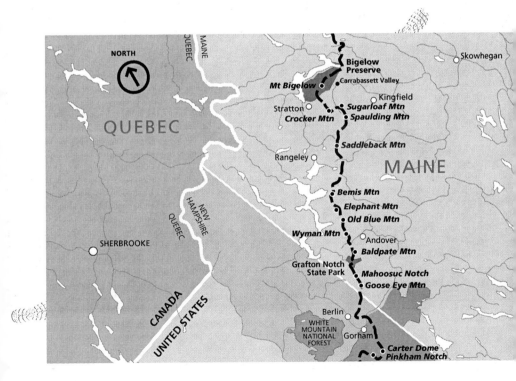

Welcome to Maine:
The Way Life Should Be

*J*UST BEFORE THE MAINE BORDER was a sign that said that portions of the trail were reconstructed in memory of a past thru-hiker. Five minutes later I was staring at a jumble of huge rocks. Jumbles of rocks weren't unusual in that section of the AT, but one 75 foot section was difficult to navigate. The crux was a flat squarish boulder that was positioned so that two of the corners looked like they were pivot points. You had to drop on one of the floating corners hoping the boulder wouldn't pivot on you. Oh, and the boulder wasn't horizontal, it was angled, so if you slipped you would slide off the other floating corner into the gap it was resting over. Was this the reconstruction they were talking about?

Shortly after I entered Maine, there was a nice "Welcome to Maine" sign on the trail. It felt good to be there. It's odd how something as arbitrary as a state line can give you such a feeling of satisfaction.

Soon the state let me know that I wouldn't be zooming through. As if to say, "You might have made it to Maine, but you haven't made it," I was presented with an 18-wheeler sized boulder that I had to shimmy down the long way. Southern Maine wouldn't be a cakewalk.

Journal Entry
August 8

THE NOTCH

Today was my shortest day on the trail so far. I've never had a single digit mileage day without it being a choice. Maine is rough, much rougher than the Whites.

The highlight of today was the Mahoosuc Notch, a 1.1 mile amusement park made of stone. It is billed as the roughest mile on the AT.

To make things more interesting, it began to rain as I entered the notch.

The notch is like a crevasse or a sharp ravine, about 100 feet wide. A river flows through it, but for the most part you can't see it, you can only hear it. This is because the river runs beneath hundreds of house-sized boulders that were sprinkled into the ravine.

The folks that maintain this section have a good sense of humor. The blazed trail goes under and over various boulders and through a few cave-like places, some just big enough for a person without a pack. Despite being tired, it was a lot of fun.

After you get out of the notch, it gets hard. Having heard about the notch for a while, I was mentally prepared for a slow mile. Nobody mentions the hike out which goes almost straight up. Today the smooth slabby trail out of the area was wet from rain. I got to the camp after the notch and decided to stay there. I spent the rest of the day eating.

Wild Flamingo had emailed me about his experience with the notch. He also got rained on as he went through. He wrote me from a place called "The Cabin" in Andover, Maine. He gave The Cabin two thumbs up. His favorite feature of The Cabin — All you can eat, all day.

The problem was that The Cabin was far off of the trail, and I don't like hitch-hiking. To make matters worse, the logical road that gets you there is gravel and not well traveled. Assuming I got a hitch, I wouldn't know how to give my ride directions to The Cabin. For the entire day I was wound up about how the hitch would go.

My hitching problems were solved while filling up my water bladder. Two hikers I hadn't seen before, Tang and Jolly Green Giant, arrived. Both were staying at The Cabin and had made plans to be picked up that evening. Jolly Green Giant was a big guy whose name fit him well. He had hiked the trail the year before but had to stop early for some reason that I never found out.

Tang got her name because a lot of her gear was orange. I did not make the connection at first, but when she mentioned how she got her name I noticed the orange backpack, orange bandanna and sunglasses with an orange tint.

I asked to tag along with them for the rest of the day, happy that I would have an easy ride to The Cabin. They were getting picked up late, so there was no sense in rushing to get to the road only to have to wait. We made an easy day hiking over the beautiful Maine landscape.

With about two miles to go we heard some frantic whistles. We came upon a group of girls from Canada who were out hiking for a week or so. One of the girls was curled up in a ball in the center of the trail. The girls spoke French with only a little English. I thought I could understand a little French, but my French turned out to be useless. The injured girl had no broken bones to splint or cuts to bandage. She had fainted, been unconscious for a while, and was now weak and in great pain. She and those around her said that she had drunk water during the day, but had not eaten much. They also mentioned that she had gone to the hospital the day before with similar symptoms but was released when they could not find anything wrong. I wasn't sure what to do.

We sent Jolly Green Giant ahead to tell the guy from The Cabin that we would be late, which in hindsight was dumb. Jolly Green Giant, like his namesake, was a big guy and could have carried the girl out over his shoulder. Tang and I decided to call 911 on Tang's cell phone and carry the girl out to meet the medical team as they came in. With Tang and me on either side, we carried the girl as best we could. It was a rough hike. I'm not a strong guy to begin with, and I was running on fumes after the Whites.

Eventually we got to where the trail split. This was a case where it would have been good to carry a map. The blue blazed trail looked easier, but we weren't sure if it went to the road. The *Data Book* told us that the white-blazed AT crossed the road for sure. So we followed the AT, which crossed a stream and went up a steep hill. We decided to rest to gather some strength for the hill. While resting the EMS team showed up.

There was now a crowd around the young girl. Tang and I decided to go back and get our packs while the medic did his thing. Exhaustion truly set in at this point. With every curve of the trail I was amazed at how far we carried her. We finally came across our stuff, gathered it up and headed back.

To our surprise, everyone was gone when we got back. We continued hiking along the AT wondering what had happened. We found out a mile later at the road crossing, where there were many vehicles, including an ambulance. In a small town like Andover, there is no shortage of help when the call goes out.

It turned out that the medic gave the girl some sugar/saline solution which worked like magic. The girl ended up walking out on her own. When we saw her she looked slightly embarrassed for causing so much trouble.

Night Runner and Cliff Dweller greeted us. Bear, the guy who runs the cabin, had sent them to wait for us. A few minutes later we arrived at The Cabin. Bear greeted us with a warm welcome as we rolled up. He told us to go up to the deck where dinner was being served and that he would take care of our packs for us.

We sat down to as many burgers, and as much salad and ice cream as we could stomach. For the next three days The Cabin would be home.

THE CABIN

Right now I'm at The Cabin watching "The Real World" marathon with Jump'n, Tang and Jolly Green Giant. Today is a zero day. It's pouring outside and the forecast doesn't look good.

I heard about The Cabin from Wild Flamingo, Medicine Man and many southbounders. They all raved about the place, and it turns out to be even better in person.

For the last week I've felt more and more tired each day. The Cabin is cozy and the perfect place to recuperate. Our hosts, Bear and Honey are extremely generous.

The question now is: How many zero days?

While I was staying at The Cabin, two other thru-hikers showed up. They smoked, stayed outside in one of the campers on the property and generally kept to themselves. Without being rude they gave me the impression that they didn't want to be bothered. They were roommates at Georgia Tech and were hiking the trail together. They were the only thru-hikers I met on the trail who didn't have trail names.

One of them had the number "13" tattooed on his shoulder, his birthday, which was on a Friday. His right leg had a tattoo of a Colt .45. The butt of the gun was on his butt, the barrel extended to just above his knee. The tattoo was huge. I asked him, "Why did you get a .45 tattooed on your leg?" With a tone that implied that I was totally ignorant he responded, "Because it's the biggest fucking revolver they've ever made." He also said that eventually he wanted to get a holster for it.

In southern Virginia these two guys encountered a section hiker who was trying to find the owner of a lost puppy. The section hiker had been unable to locate the owner and offered these tough looking guys the puppy. They declined, but later regretted it as they walked on. Through some odd hiking schedule that section hikers sometimes follow, they met again. This time "13" and his friend accepted the puppy and named it Caddy. These two tough guys hiking with Caddy, their beautiful Malamute puppy made for a unique site.

Caddy was well behaved, most of the time. At one point the trio was hopping rocks to cross one of the many streams in Maine. Caddy made the mistake of knocking "13," causing him to lose his balance and fall into the stream, getting firmly dunked. If I had caused "13" to go into the river I'd expect to be buried somewhere just off of the trail. But he loved Caddy and after Caddy was vigorously baptized, they were even.

STILL AT THE CABIN

Tonight is my third night at The Cabin. The Cabin is hard to leave.

Yesterday, five of us took a zero day. In the morning we watched a movie in our apartment. Jolly Green Giant spent the day cooking dinner and Jump'n, Cliff Dweller, Tang and I split wood. After splitting wood we borrowed Bear's truck and drove down to a nearby covered bridge to hang out by the river. A relaxing day for our feet and legs. We continued to eat big. I've gained seven pounds since I arrived here.

A few folks arrived during the day, and we had a full table for dinner.

Today we all got back on the trail to get some hiking in. Only Jump'n, Tang and I planned on returning to The Cabin.

Tang and I enjoyed an easy hike over an easy ten miles. No slippery ledges, no house sized boulders, just a normal trail through the woods.

Bear arrived early to pick us up. With his persuasive style he lured four of us back. Only Cliff Dweller had the will to pass up another night at The Cabin.

I hiked about 20 miles with Tang during our stay at The Cabin. This formed a habit that would continue for the next couple of hundred miles.

Once we left and were back on the trail, we decided to re-supply in Stratton. This required hitchhiking again, which I hate doing. I had put some thought into hitching and had a system. Whenever I wanted to hitch, I would primp my dirty unshowered self as much as possible, take off my hat, and collapse my hiking poles, all in an effort to look less intimidating. I would also walk to a section of road where cars could see me and would have a reasonable area to pull off.

Tang had a different hitching style. While I was messing with my poles I saw her drop her pack, sit on it, and put her thumb out. We were on a curve, not a good spot. If a car saw us, they'd have to make a quick decision to pick us up, and if they did decide to pick us up there was not a good place to pull over. I considered mentioning a few of my "tips" to Tang in order to improve our chances. Before I could get a word out, I discovered the power of a tall blond in a skirt.

While I was thinking of whether I should have my hat on or off, the first pick-up that passed by screeched to a halt. First car. Amazing. We tossed our packs in and were invited into the front.

While hiking with Tang, hitchhiking was no longer a problem. It opened up a new form of public transportation. It was like magic. She just sat on her pack, put her thumb out, and voila, a friendly ride stopped.

Tang

SADDLEBACK

We've had nice weather the last couple of days. Today we went over Saddleback Mountain. The Companion *says that you can see Katahdin on a good day. There was a slight haze, but if you used your imagination you could see where the AT ends.*

Jump'n, Tang, Jolly Green Giant and I have stuck together since The Cabin. It's nice to see the same people from camp to camp for a few nights. Jump'n is fast and usually has a fire going when Tang and I roll in. Jolly Green Giant arrives towards dark.

Jolly Green Giant has been pushing himself to hike the miles we are hiking. We aren't doing any huge miles, but his third 20-mile day (ever) was yesterday. He's nice to have around but he may be pushing himself a bit and that might catch up with him.

We are getting close to the end. There are only 200 miles to go. There have been times when I see a southbounder and feel like my sentence is almost up, and they are just starting theirs. Then there are times when I'm sad because the trail is running out.

Lately though, being in Maine, with the nice weather, I feel like telling them to quit after Maine, it all goes downhill from there. Maine has become my favorite state.

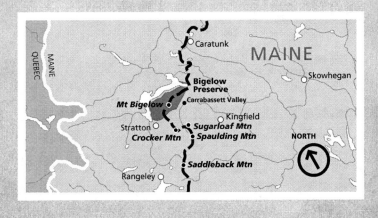

THOUSANDS OF MILES

Today we passed the 2,000-mile mark. Again, like a birthday, nothing really changes. The "mark" was actually painted on a road. Jump'n, Tang and I took pictures next to it, being careful to not get run over.

We decided our next town stop will be Caratunk, Maine, and that we should take three days to get there. Yesterday we did five miles. I was thinking about going further, but that would mean camping out by myself, but still getting into Caratunk at the same time. So I settled on a five-mile day.

The shelter was right near a glacial pond and some of us hung out on the edge to take in the Northwoods scenery. Some hikers in the shelter were from Maine so I quizzed them about Maine stuff.

The pond has trout, which is not natural since it has no moving water. It turns out that they carry up a bunch of chilled baby trout in backpacks. They used to use the traditional method, a helicopter, but had problems. Since the pond is at the top of a mountain, there are some odd wind currents, and apparently the fish would end up on land instead of in the water. One time the fish were blown up into the helicopter blades. At least that's what the locals say.

One of the caretakers at the shelter was from out West. She moved to Maine for her man, but what he didn't know was that her job as caretaker has her at the shelter 10 out of 14 days. The shelter is a three-hour hike from the nearest road.

Today we hiked through the Bigelows, a popular range of mountains. The skies cleared and it ended up being a pretty lazy day despite a lot of ups and downs. From here on out the going is supposed to be flat and easy.

LAZY DAYS

Today we decided to hike only 13 miles. At the end of the day we crossed the Kennebec River. The river is dangerous to ford and there is a ferry, but in the afternoon the ferry only runs from 3:00 p.m. to 5:00 p.m. So the day wouldn't be rushed.

I slept in. By the time I got up and walked around, everyone was long gone except for Tang. After taking forever to eat breakfast and pack up, we finally hit the trail.

Maine has a lot of lakes. About an hour into the hike we came across a sandy beach on one of them. After an hour over completely flat terrain we needed a break so we hung out there for a while. Our very lazy day was getting lazier.

We ended up getting to the ferry with half an hour to spare. Another half mile of hiking completed the lazy day.

We're at Caratunk House now. It's a B&B. There are six of us in the loft. The loft has six beds, a sofa, a TV and a bunch of movies. Plenty to keep hikers entertained and out of the way of the B&B guests.

The end is getting close now, only 10 or so days left.

Where is Everyone?

WHILE AT CARATUNK HOUSE, I saw Hoser's picture in a photo album. I forgot the exact date, but I heard he finished the AT earlier in the month. Wild Flamingo finished a few days later on August 8. I emailed Mr. Ed's mom and found out that he was a few days behind me in Maine.

Journal Entry
August 19

SAD

Today I realized I'll be done soon. I've known I am going to finish at the end of the month, but today it really hit me. It made me sad.

The weather was perfect, with sunshine and low humidity. The terrain was easy, and the wilderness was amazing. These are the days I'll miss the most. Today the end was in sight, literally, since you can see Katahdin from the mountain tops if you squint just right.

It seemed silly to be sad on such a great day, so I decided to postpone those feelings until after I'm off the trail.

For some reason I started to visualize my first days back. I thought about the things I'd do with all my free time. I realized I had no plans, no agenda, no list of things to do. That was a little scary, so I postponed those thoughts too.

Maine is nice. It helps that the weather is perfect and that the terrain has become easy. The climbs are less frequent and shorter, and there are countless lakes, most with sandy beaches. Maine is a great place to be.

Tomorrow we're going to Monson, Maine. Monson is a town at the southern end of the 100-Mile Wilderness. Katahdin is at the northern end. We are getting close.

The next day, after eating lunch, Tang and I encountered two very agitated Dobermans who ran up to us on the trail. We started to backtrack down the trail, but every step we made backwards seemed to get the dogs more angry. Luckily, they were more into barking than biting and the pair remained a trekking pole's distance away.

After a few moments of barking, we heard a lady's voice. She was swimming in a lake just off the trail. She called her dogs, but they didn't respond at all. We asked her to please get her dogs since her calls didn't seem to do anything.

She replied that she couldn't get out of the water because she was naked and did not want us to see her. I considered telling her that we would close our eyes while she came and got her dogs, or that we would look the other way, but I started to get angry. Regardless of what we did, the lady needed to get her dogs. Before she stripped down, she should have thought about what might happen if she left them next to the trail.

It finally dawned on Tang and me that we were between the woman and the Dobermans. We slowly stepped off of the trail, away from the dogs and away from the lake. The dogs took the opening and ran down to their naked owner, who still hadn't made a move to get out of the water.

JUMP'N IN THE RAIN

Tang and I are taking a break at a shelter right now. Jump'n was here waking up from a nap when we arrived but he left about ten minutes ago. We're planning on hiking another two miles to meet him at a campsite. Now it's starting to rain.

Tang and I will probably hike on, even if it's raining, to keep Jump'n company. Probably.

The weather has been odd today. The skies were clear when we woke up. We hiked up Chairback Mountain and had another view of Katahdin.

As we walked it started to cloud up. We planned on hiking a side trail that loops up and down a gorge with a few waterfalls, but the place was packed with people. In the middle of the 100-Mile Wilderness we saw a dozen groups.

Between the parking lot and the trail is a river. We stopped to put our Waldies on before walking through the water. While we were changing back into our shoes on the other side, we watched groups ford the river. A few crossed in long pants (that got wet of course). One carried a box of doughnuts (just one box?). It was fun to watch the people, but not what I expected in the "100-Mile Wilderness."

The rain has stopped, so Jump'n is probably okay (and we might leave the shelter).

Right now we are less than 80 miles from Katahdin. At this time next week I won't be hiking.

MOOSE

I wouldn't normally write so soon (only three hours after the last entry), but we saw a moose.

Despite the bad weather, we left the shelter. A few minutes later Tang spotted a moose in a marshy pond. The trail curved around the pond, and we took a side trail for a closer look.

The moose kept its eye on us, but didn't move much, until we got too close. Then it ran through the woods to its calf, which we hadn't seen.

That was our first moose sighting. Almost everyone else has seen moose and some local people we talked to said they see Moose regularly from their cars. Now we can say we've seen one too.

Now I'm in my hammock. It's windy, cold (45 degrees and it's only 6:30 p.m.) and drizzly. Not fun. My hands are cold as I type this, and the trees that my hammock is tied to are swaying in the wind. One of the trees looks dead in places and might fall in the night. I can picture it falling, wanting to fall safely away from me, but being pulled directly toward me by the tension in the hammock's lines. If I get crushed by that falling tree, let it be known that it was because I was too lazy to go out in the cold and move my hammock.

I can't believe we left the shelter for this!

The weather wasn't much better in the morning, but at least the trees my hammock was anchored to didn't fall. I was relieved, but cold. The cold morning prodded Tang, Jump'n and me off to an early start. Our day began with a climb, which warmed me up nicely. Hiking is the best part of the day, especially when it's cold out.

After a few ups and downs we found ourselves at the top of Whitecap Mountain. For days we had been trying to spy the big "K," trying to pick out which of the many distant mountains it might be. There was no mistaking it from the top of Whitecap. With only rolling hills between Whitecap and Katahdin, it stood out. Like a volcano, it emerged from the surrounding hills and stretched upward into the clouds.

On the way down Whitecap we stopped for lunch at a shelter. A family of southbound day hikers arrived and told us that they encountered some bees on the trail. They told us that the bees would be around some specially shaped tree.

Hiking out of the shelter I quickly forgot about the bee story and lost interest in inspecting the hundreds of trees in the forest for some vaguely described special shape. Toward the bottom of the long descent, Tang got stung on the back of her calf. Normally, Tang betrays her blond stereotype with rare intelligence, wit and common sense, but on this day she immediately stopped to swat at the bees swarming around our legs.

They have a saying on the trail, "Hike Your Own Hike" which I fully subscribe to. So if Tang wants to stop in the trail and inspect her sting while bees are buzzing around, that's fine with me, she can hike her own hike. But we were together and she was in front of me blocking the logical escape route. I was not yet stung, and hoping to keep it that way. With a few kind words and a gentle push on her pack we both took off.

The bee sting left a pretty good mark, much worse than my own bee encounter in Vermont. We hiked on. Tang was tough and only brought up how much the bee sting hurt every mile or so.

Jump'n, Tang and I were now getting close to the end of the trail. In camp we would talk about what post-trail life would be. We had all heard that the transition from trail-life to real-life was sometimes hard.

JUST LIKE HOME

Based on this evening, I think my transition back to non-trail life will be effortless.

Tang and I are at White House Landing. White House Landing is a camp in the middle of the 100-Mile Wilderness set on a large lake. The bunkhouse is all windows on the lakeside and provides a wide view of the lake as well as mountains we've gone over recently.

To get here we walked a mile off the trail and gave one blast on an air horn. About ten minutes later we saw someone moving around on the other side of the lake. Soon a boat was headed our way. I was starving, but we got here during the caretaker's naptime, so I had to wait an hour to eat.

Dinner was the biggest cheeseburger I've ever seen, which was followed by a pint of Ben & Jerry's ice cream.

We have the bunkhouse to ourselves. The wood-burning stove is going (it's still cold). We each have a couch to ourselves to spread out on to nap or read. Not too different than what I do in real life.

I remember being in Pennsylvania where I hit the halfway point and was overwhelmed that after all the walking and all the time, I was only half way. The trail seemed so long that day. Now, with 46 miles to go, I wonder where all of the miles went.

Forty-six miles seemed so close. The mentality I had for most of the trail would have seen 46 miles as a two-day hike. The White Mountains pulverized that way of thinking, and Maine's Mahoosic Notch all but finished it off.

While at The Cabin I got to know Tang and Jump'n and after leaving The Cabin we made plans every morning to camp at the same shelter or campsite that night. Initially after leaving The Cabin we hiked a few 20 mile days —a compromise between Tang, who wanted to relax and enjoy the hike through Maine, and the remnants of my mile-obsessed thinking.

Slowly we did fewer and fewer miles each day. Why get to Monson in two days when you can get there in three? The easy pace and good company complemented Maine's wild beauty. Sleeping in and long lunches became the norm.

Between the 100-Mile Wilderness and the entrance to Baxter State Park, where the northern end of the trail lies, is Abol Bridge. Abol Bridge has a campground. The campground is more suited for RVs, but we had no problem calling it home for the night.

A week or so earlier, I decided that I was close enough to the end of the trail that I could send home some things that I wouldn't need any longer. One of the items I sent home was a pair of warm gloves. I regretted it immediately and decided to get some new gloves at the camp store at Abol Bridge. They had a very limited selection. I finally settled on what I thought would be the warmest, a pair of fuzzy, bright yellow work gloves. They would keep me warm the rest of the trail.

While at Abol Bridge, with a lot of time to kill, Jump'n, Tang and I decided to hitchhike into Millinocket. We did not really need anything there; it was more of a challenge to see if we could hitchhike out of the middle of nowhere.

For a moment it looked like the logging trucks were deaf to Tang's hitching prowess — something about "company rules." But the rules proved to be no match for Tang and soon the three of us were packed into an 18-wheel truck that was loaded sky high with giant logs.

There wasn't much to do in Millinocket. We ate and then stopped by the post office. My last mail-drop had arrived, so I took it back to Abol Bridge. I opened it and found that the box contained a cake stuffed into a Tupperware container. The cake had suffered a little during the trip, but after a moment we were able to make out "Congratulations Iron Toothpick" written in frosting. I knew what to do. I saved the cake for the summit of Katahdin to enjoy it there.

The next morning we hiked into Baxter State Park. The end of the trail is in the park, at the top of Mt. Katahdin. Baxter State Park is famous for being incredibly hard to get into. In order to keep the wilderness wild, Maine limits the number of people who can visit the park and reservations, which are difficult to get, have to be made months in advance.

This would present a serious problem for thru-hikers, but the folks at Baxter State Park understand our cause. They have a walk-in campsite called the Birches that is just for us.

We arrived at the Birches in time to talk to a few thru-hikers who reached the summit that day. They told us how they were rained on, how it was very cold, how the climb up the Big K was the hardest climb of the trail, and how incredibly great it felt to be at the northern terminus of the AT.

I was envious and apprehensive. I'm not sure what I thought would prevent me from making the final six-mile hike, but I felt nervous. Would the weather be miserable? Would the trail be too difficult? Would I make it?

On paper the final six miles of the trail are the hardest, but the reality is that they are all "easies." I woke up on the final morning and packed all my gear for one last hike on the AT.

THE TRAIL ENDED!?

At this time yesterday we were starting the last leg of the AT. We wanted to get a head start on the day hikers and have the summit all to ourselves. The following people were present at the start: Bob-Mike-Bob, Jump'n, Tang, Phoenix, Tang's dad, and Phoenix's parents.

While we were taking pictures at the trailhead two day hikers passed. Ugh. We all signed in, which took a while, and then left.

I had my "full" pack, although I didn't have much food and water so it was the lightest it has ever been. With a light pack and a fun route up the mountain, I easily flew over the ground.

It was the most challenging climb of the trip, but it was also the last climb. Everything was easy. I'd approach a gigantic boulder face blocking the way and think "how am I going to get up this?" and without stopping just go up it. At the top I'd glance back and wonder how I just did that. Every movement was effortless.

As we approached the summit, the trees became shorter, and I stopped to look around and take it all in. Mother Nature delivered the best weather of this trip, which seems to be a tall order in Maine. Unlimited visibility, very high clouds, and cool temperatures. I could see forever.

I'd stop occasionally and snap pictures of Bob-Mike-Bob or of Jump'n who were near me most of the climb.

The climb went above the tree-line and only got better with tougher scrambling and more expansive views. The route led up to a well-defined ridge and then followed the ridge to the "Table Top."

Where the ridge ended at the edge of the flat Table Top was a sign that said to stay on the trail. It had some long explanation about why it was good to stay on the trail. The wordy sign was large and from a distance it looked like pictures I had seen of the sign at the peak of Katahdin. I knew what I had to do.

I broke out of my goofing off pace and sprinted toward the top. With the others still behind I stood behind the sign with my hands up in celebration. At least one person fell for it.

From the Table Top we still had 45 minutes of easy walking to the summit. It went by quickly enough. Jump'n and I stopped before the very top to wait for Tang, who had hiked the first bit with her dad. Then team Jump'n, Tang, Phoenix (new member), and Iron Toothpick hiked to the famous sign at the top.

Once there, we all took pictures around the sign and hung out for an hour or so. We even ate a little of the "Congratulations" cake.

Three out of four team members wanted to descend on the so-called "Knife Edge." I had planned on getting back down the easiest way possible, and the "Knife Edge" didn't sound like the easiest way.

For me, climbing any mountain is enjoyable, but the real satisfaction comes at the bottom when you can relax and bask in your accomplishment. So, having this attitude, I think it is very important to make it down alive since the bottom is where the good part is. On this day I caved to peer pressure and took the "Knife Edge" route down.

The wind kicked up and made me a little more nervous. It turned out though, that the "Knife Edge" is easy and there is never any danger of falling to your death. It was pretty gusty which made keeping my balance tougher, but that only added to the challenge, not to the level of danger.

Hikers coming up reported that it was only windy on the last bit (the first bit for us). What was actually happening was that the wind was getting stronger as the day went on. By the time we reached the end of the ridge the wind was ridiculous. You could lean into it with your full weight. The sand and pebbles formed drifts around your feet like at the beach. It was a little unpleasant. The kind of experience that stinks when you are going through it, but you laugh about when you are done.

The AT ends at the top of the mountain. So at the top we were done. The route down was simply extra credit. Our first day hike after completing the AT.

View from Mt. Katahdin summit

Freedom

*I*N VIRGINIA, HOSER AND I TALKED ABOUT not hiking the final several hundred feet of the AT. Our plan was to hike to the top, and 200 feet short of the wooden sign that marks the northern end, we would turn around, leaving our thru-hike forever unfinished. We'd mention our plan to other thru-hikers and they'd look at us in disbelief. It was clear most people planned on embracing the giant wooden sign that marks the end of the trail like a long lost lover.

Hoser finished a month ahead of me and, as far as I know, he completed the last few feet of the trail. On a different day, perhaps a day when Hoser was around, I might have turned around, leaving some token amount of the trail unfinished. As it happened, I walked to the sign and posed next to it for the standard Katahdin photos.

Feelings of happiness and satisfaction poured over me, but not in the copious amounts that I expected. When I started the trail I was both certain I would finish and scared that I would not. In Damascus, with a fourth of the trail behind me, I knew that completing a thru-hike was in my future. If something happened to me, I would come back the next year, if something happened the next year, I'd be back the year after. I visualized a thru-hike of the AT becoming a dangerous obsession in my life. After a month, the AT had firmly sunk its teeth into me.

During my two-week hiatus from the trail, I thought about returning to the trail every moment. With no responsibilities, I would contemplate driving out to the trail to hike a few miles and driving back home. I decided not to visit the AT during my hiatus, not because I came to my senses, but because I decided that leaving from my house, hiking a bit, and returning to my house, would violate my arbitrary definition of a thru-hike.

I returned from my two-week vacation from the trail and saw many familiar faces. Along with those faces came stories of those who had dropped off of the trail. Those stories of family emergencies, worn-out knees, and stress fractures increased my fear of not completing what I had set out to do. At no time did I feel that I couldn't make it, but I always feared that I wouldn't.

This fed my obsession with mileage. More miles meant more of a cushion. If something did happen to me, I would not have as far to hike when I returned to the trail. I visualized how I would handle various scenarios. I'd wonder how many miles I could hike a day if I had a cast on. Every town I passed near would prompt me to determine how I would return to that town if I had to leave the trail. Was there a bus station? How close was the closest airport? How long would it take to drive there? I was focused.

The greatest emotion I felt on the day I reached the top of Katahdin was relief. All tension in my body disappeared, I could finally relax — the trail was complete. No more worries about freak injuries. So what if I contracted some mysterious illness, I had finished the trail. This bewildered me a bit. It felt out of place that my greatest emotion for finishing the trail was relief. I felt that finishing should have been a tremendous emotional experience.

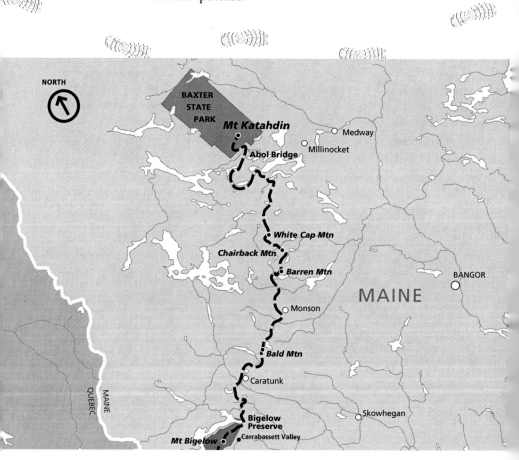

BABY STEPS

My transition back to my old life is going well. I just finished my first post-trail Frosty.

We just dropped Jump'n off, somewhere outside of Concord, New Hampshire. I'm about to nap in the back of Tang's minivan.

The minivan is in road-trip mode and looks a bit like a yard sale. The seats are out and there are packs and stuff everywhere. There is even an old three-speed bike in the back that was actually purchased at a real yard sale in Millinocket this morning.

This morning we ate breakfast with team Bob-Mike-Bob at the Appalachian Trail Cafe. I didn't eat much, I think my body knows it'll be relaxing for a bit.

After breakfast we stopped at the department store in Millinocket. It was small but I got a whole new set of clothes — all of them cotton.

Not much else happened. Just hours of driving, and of course a Wendy's stop.

In the back of Tang's minivan, somewhere in New Hampshire

My transition back to real life was made easier by Tang, her father, and her aunt and uncle. Tang's dad drove Jump'n, Tang and me south. We dropped Jump'n near his grandparents' house and continued to Tang's aunt and uncle's place in Massachusetts.

I planned on staying in Massachusetts for a few days. It was good to be in civilization with someone I shared the trail with, although at times it seemed like a string of zero days. The idea that I was off of the trail was sinking in slowly.

When I arrived at Tang's aunt and uncle's house, I had only the vaguest of plans of how I would get home. I did not have a firm date that I would be picked up, and I'm sure after a couple of days they wondered how long I would stay.

During my stay, Tang and I drove to Dalton. We were hoping to meet a few thru-hikers, but it was late in the season and in Dalton it had thinned out. We chatted with the guy who owned the place Bluegrasshopper told me about and looked through his photo album for folks we had hiked with.

The next day Tang's uncle took us to a minor league baseball game. The weather was perfect. My mind was still far away from home and far away from any kind of responsibility.

My friend Sarah drove up from New York to pick me up from Tang's—probably to the relief of Tang's aunt and uncle. That night at Sarah's house, she cooked pizza for her fiancé George and me. I realized how big my appetite was when Sarah and George, both professional athletes, were done eating, and I was nowhere near full.

The next day Sarah drove me home to Virginia. She drove more miles in a couple of days shuttling me around the northeast than I had hiked during the past five months and made me feel that she was happy to do it. I can't thank her enough.

For me, the full experience of the trail extended far beyond Maine. The day I finished the trail I felt that the trip was complete. I have since learned that the end of the trail is really just the beginning.

I immediately looked for the trail's impact on my personality. I failed to see anything significant until many months had passed. I can now tell that I see people differently. Not better or worse, just different. I see ads on TV differently; amazed at the techniques used to sell products, and amazed when I sense that they might be working on me.

My vantage point on life has been gently lifted, and I feel that I see the terrain around me with more clarity. I see decisions that have always been there, but were previously obscured as I let my life's momentum roll over them. I can now see the lay of the land that is my life and decisions are more obvious and easier to make. Whereas before I was on the ground, now I'm just above the trees. What a difference a hundred feet of altitude makes on what you can see.

The trail trained me in the simple life. It was a playground that showed me that the simple life is safe. It taught me that strangers are friends. It taught me more respect for nature, respect for the rare havoc she is capable of and respect for the calm nurturing environment that she provides most of the time.

I do not believe that there is anything uniquely special about the Appalachian Trail that provides these lessons. The Appalachian Trail just happens to be where I went to school. There must be countless schools. I believe that any endeavor that allows one to focus their life, even for a short period, will do. The longer the better. A lifetime of focus would be best.

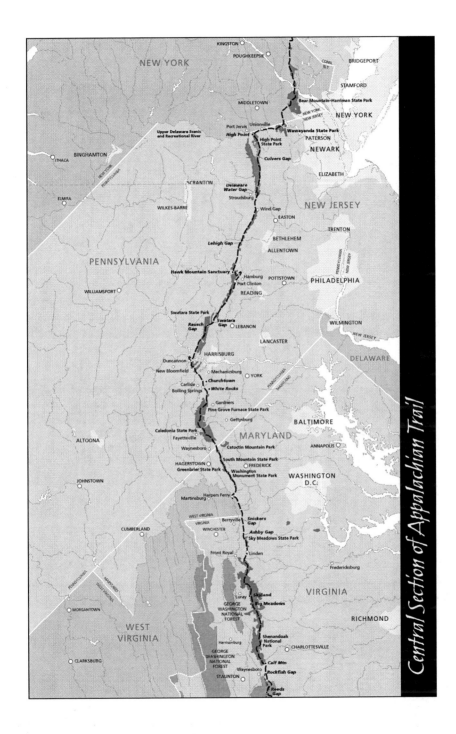

Central Section of Appalachian Trail

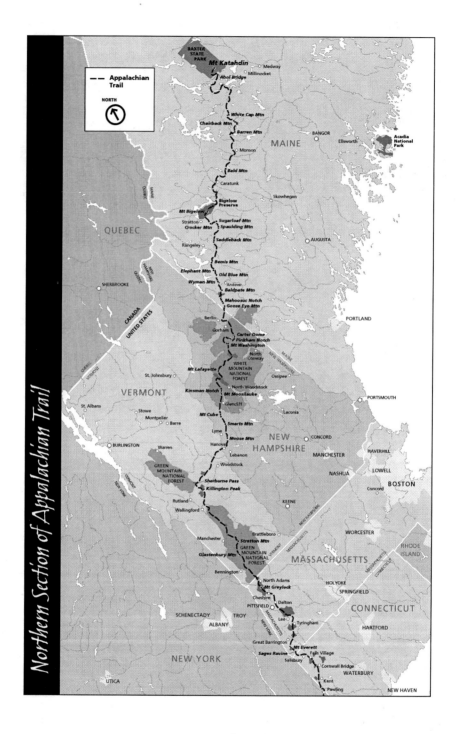